THE INTERNATIONAL ANNUAL OF PHOTOGRAPHY

DAS INTERNATIONALE JAHRBUCH DER PHOTOGRAPHIE

LE RÉPERTOIRE INTERNATIONAL DE LA PHOTOGRAPHIE

EDITED BY · HERAUSGEGEBEN VON · REALISÉ PAR:

B. MARTIN PEDERSEN

PUBLISHER AND CREATIVE DIRECTOR: B. MARTIN PEDERSEN

EDITORS: HEINKE JENSSEN, ANNETTE CRANDALL

ART DIRECTORS: B. MARTIN PEDERSEN, ADRIAN PULFER

DESIGNERS: MARY JANE CALLISTER, ERIC GILLETT, ADRIAN PULFER

GRAPHIS PRESS CORP. ZÜRICH (SWITZERLAND)

GRAPHIS PUBLICATIONS

GRAPHIS, THE INTERNATIONAL BI-MONTHLY JOURNAL OF VISUAL COMMUNICATION

GRAPHIS DESIGN, THE INTERNATIONAL ANNUAL OF DESIGN AND ILLUSTRATION

GRAPHIS PHOTO, THE INTERNATIONAL ANNUAL OF PHOTOGRAPHY

GRAPHIS POSTER, THE INTERNATIONAL ANNUAL OF POSTER ART

GRAPHIS PACKAGING, AN INTERNATIONAL SURVEY OF PACKACKING DESIGN

GRAPHIS LETTERHEAD, AN INTERNATIONAL SURVEY OF LETTERHEAD DESIGN

GRAPHIS DIAGRAM, THE GRAPHIC VISUALIZATION OF ABSTRACT, TECHNICAL AND STATISTICAL FACTS AND FUNCTIONS

GRAPHIS LOGO, AN INTERNATIONAL SURVEY OF LOGOS

GRAPHIS PUBLICATION, AN INTERNATIONAL SURVEY OF THE BEST IN MAGAZINE DESIGN

GRAPHIS ANNUAL REPORTS, AN INTERNATIONAL COMPILATION OF THE BEST DESIGNED ANNUAL REPORTS

GRAPHIS CORPORATE IDENTITY, AN INTERNATIONAL COMPILATION OF THE BEST IN CORPORATE IDENTITY DESIGN

ART FOR SURVIVAL: THE ILLUSTRATOR AND THE ENVIRONMENT, A DOCUMENT OF ART IN THE SERVICE OF MAN.

THE GRAPHIC DESIGNER'S GREEN BOOK, ENVIRONMENTAL CONCEPTS OF THE DESIGN AND PRINT INDUSTRIES

GRAPHIS PUBLIKATIONEN

GRAPHIS, DIE INTERNATIONALE ZWEIMONATSZEITSCHRIFT DER VISUELLEN KOMMUNIKATION

GRAPHIS DESIGN, DAS INTERNATIONALE JAHRBUCH ÜBER DESIGN UND ILLUSTRATION

GRAPHIS PHOTO, DAS INTERNATIONALE JAHRBUCH DER PHOTOGRAPHIE

GRAPHIS POSTER, DAS INTERNATIONALE JAHRBUCH DER PLAKATKUNST

GRAPHIS PACKAGING, EIN INTERNATIONALER ÜBERBLICK ÜBER DIE PACKUNGSGESTALTUNG

GRAPHIS LETTERHEAD, EIN INTERNATIONALER ÜBERBLICK ÜBER BRIEFPAPIERGESTALTUNG

GRAPHIS DIAGRAM, DIE GRAPHISCHE DARSTELLUNG ABSTRAKTER TECHNISCHER UND STATISTISCHER DATEN UND FAKTEN

GRAPHIS LOGO, EINE INTERNATIONALE AUSWAHL VON FIRMEN-LOGOS

GRAPHIS MAGAZINDESIGN, EINE INTERNATIONALE ZUSAMMENSTELLUNG DES BESTEN ZEITSCHRIFTEN-DESIGNS

GRAPHIS ANNUAL REPORTS, EIN INTERNATIONALER ÜBERBLICK ÜBER DIE GESTALTUNG VON JAHRESBERICHTEN

GRAPHIS CORPORATE IDENTITY, EINE INTERNATIONALE AUSWAHL DES BESTEN CORPORATE IDENTITY DESIGNS

ART FOR SURVIVAL: THE ILLUSTRATOR AND THE ENVIRONMENT, EIN DOKUMENT ÜBER DIE KUNST IM DIENSTE DES MENSCHEN

THE GRAPHIC DESIGNER'S GREEN BOOK, UMWELTKONZEPTE DER DESIGN- UND DRUCKINDUSTRIE

PUBLICATIONS GRAPHIS

GRAPHIS, LA REVUE BIMESTRIELLE INTERNATIONALE DE LA COMMUNICATION VISUELLE

GRAPHIS DESIGN, LE RÉPERTOIRE INTERNATIONAL DE LA COMMUNICATION VISUELLE

GRAPHIS PHOTO, LE RÉPERTOIRE INTERNATIONAL DE LA PHOTOGRAPHIE

GRAPHIS POSTER, LE RÉPERTOIRE INTERNATIONAL DE L'AFFICHE

GRAPHIS PACKAGING, LE RÉPERTOIRE INTERNATIONAL DE LA CRÉATION D'EMBALLAGES

GRAPHIS LETTERHEAD, LE RÉPERTOIRE INTERNATIONAL DU DESIGN DE PAPIER À LETTRES

GRAPHIS DIAGRAM, LE RÉPERTOIRE GRAPHIQUE DE FAITS ET DONNÉES ABSTRAITS, TECHNIQUES ET STATISTIQUES

GRAPHIS LOGO, LE RÉPERTOIRE INTERNATIONAL DU LOGO

GRAPHIS PUBLICATION, LE RÉPERTOIRE INTERNATIONAL DU DESIGN DE PÉRIODIQUES

GRAPHIS ANNUAL REPORTS, PANORAMA INTERNATIONAL DU MEILLEUR DESIGN DE RAPPORTS ANNUELS D'ENTREPRISES

GRAPHIS CORPORATE IDENTITY, PANORAMA INTERNATIONAL DU MEILLEUR DESIGN D'IDENTITÉ CORPORATE

ART FOR SURVIVAL: THE ILLUSTRATOR AND THE ENVIRONMENT, L'ART AU SERVICE DE LA SURVIE

THE GRAPHIC DESIGNER'S GREEN BOOK, L'ÉCOLOGIE APPLIQUÉE AU DESIGN ET À L'INDUSTRIE GRAPHIQUE

PUBLICATION NO. 211 (ISBN 3-85709-292-0)
© COPYRIGHT UNDER UNIVERSAL COPYRIGHT CONVENTION
COPYRIGHT © 1992 BY GRAPHIS PRESS CORP., DUFOURSTRASSE 107, 8008 ZURICH, SWITZERLAND
JACKET AND BOOK DESIGN COPYRIGHT © 1992 BY PEDERSEN DESIGN
141 LEXINGTON AVENUE, NEW YORK, N.Y. 10016 USA
FRENCH CAPTIONS BY NICOLE VIAUD

PRINTED IN JAPAN BY TOPPAN PRINTING CO., LTD.

CONTENTS · INHALT · SOMMAIRE

AUSTRALIA ....AUS	AUSTRALIEN ....AUS	ALLEMAGNE ....GER
DENMARK ....DEN	DÄNEMARK ....DEN	AUSTRALIE ....AUS
GERMANY ....GER	DEUTSCHLAND ....GER	CANADA ....CAN
FRANCE ....FRA	FRANKREICH ....FRA	DANEMARK ....DEN
GREAT BRITAIN ....GBR	GROSSBRITANNIEN ....GBR	ETATS-UNIS ....USA
HONG KONG ....HKG	HONGKONG ....HKG	FRANCE ....FRA
ISRAEL ....ISR	ISRAEL ....ISR	GRANDE-BRETAGNE ....GBR
ITALY ....ITA	ITALIEN ....ITA	HONG KONG ....HKG
JAPAN ....JPN	JAPAN ....JPN	ISRAEL ....ISR
YUGOSLAVIA ....YUG	JUGOSLAWIEN ....YUG	ITALIE ....ITA
CANADA ....CAN	KANADA ....CAN	JAPON ....JPN
LITHUANIA ....LIT	LITAUEN ....LIT	LITUANIE ....LIT
NETHERLANDS ....NLD	NIEDERLANDE ....NLD	NORVÈGE ....NOR
NORWAY ....NOR	NORWEGEN ....NOR	PAYS-BAS ....NLD
PORTUGAL ....POR	PORTUGAL ....POR	PORTUGAL ....POR
SWEDEN ....SWE	SCHWEDEN ....SWE	SUÈDE ....SWE
SWITZERLAND ....SWI	SCHWEIZ ....SWI	SUISSE ....SWI
USA ....USA	USA ....USA	YOUGOSLAVIE ....YUG

REMARKS

WE EXTEND OUR HEARTFELT THANKS TO CONTRIBUTORS TROUGHOUT THE WORLD WHO HAVE MADE IT POSSIBLE FOR US TO PUBLISH A WIDE AND INTERNATIONAL SPECTRUM OF THE BEST WORK IN THIS FIELD.

ENTRY INSTRUCTIONS MAY BE REQUESTED AT:
GRAPHIS PRESS CORP.,
DUFOURSTRASSE 107,
8008 ZÜRICH, SWITZERLAND

ANMERKUNGEN

UNSER DANK GILT DEN EINSENDERN AUS ALLER WELT, DIE ES UNS DURCH IHRE BEITRÄGE ERMÖGLICHT HABEN, EIN BREITES, INTERNATIONALES SPEKTRUM DER BESTEN ARBEITEN ZU VERÖFFENTLICHEN.

TEILNAHMEBEDINGUNGEN:
GRAPHIS VERLAG AG,
DUFOURSTRASSE 107,
8008 ZÜRICH, SCHWEIZ

ANNOTATIONS

TOUTE NOTRE RECONNAISSANCE VA AUX PHOTOGRAPHES DU MONDE ENTIER DONT LES ENVOIS NOUS ONT PERMIS DE CONSTITUER UN VASTE PANORAMA INTERNATIONAL DES MEILLEURS TRAVAUX.

MODALITÉS D'ENVOI DE TRAVAUX:
GRAPHIS VERLAG AG,
DUFOURSTRASSE 107,
8008 ZÜRICH, SUISSE

MICHAEL O'BRIEN

. . . .

Since boyhood, I have been an outsider—more comfortable observing, dreaming from a distance, than participating. Even now, when sitting across the room from others, I remember more clearly what I see and feel than what I hear: how the light strikes their faces, revealing youth giving way to age, or the opposite; moods; how expressions change with words. But images pass, and I grieve that those instants and the feelings they hold are gone. The camera preserves what time erases. ▫ I have always been drawn to photographing people. For me, this is what the camera is for. From the beginning, when I used my camera to approach someone who intrigued me, I was hooked. Before photography, I hung on the periphery, watching; with my camera, I became involved. ▫ My work has given me access to people and places I would never have seen otherwise: an Australian stockman, a homeless man living in an Arizona riverbed, the country music star Willie Nelson. My vocation has taken me across my country and around the world. ▫ My subjects often look at the camera— direct and immediate. It is interesting—and essential—to see them address the camera, to let their eyes meet the lens on their own terms. Focusing in the ground glass, I can feel the connection or its absence. I often sense something when I make a good picture: A connection is made,

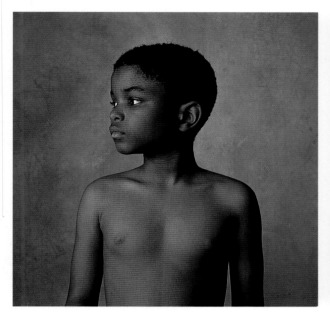 

(ABOVE LEFT) CLIENT: *LIFE* MAGAZINE DESCRIPTION: PORTRAIT OF A YOUNG BOY/PORTRÄT EINES KNABEN/PORTRAIT D'UN JEUNE GARÇON ■ (ABOVE RIGHT) CLIENT: *LIFE* MAGAZINE DESCRIPTION: PHOTOGRAPH OF A MAN IN A TEXAS BARBERSHOP/MANN IN EINEM FRISÖRGESCHAFT IN TEXAS/UN HOMME CHEZ UN COIFFEUR DU TEXAS ■ (OPPOSITE) CLIENT: *FORTUNE* MAGAZINE DESCRIPTION: PHOTO OF THE BACK OF A HOMELESS MAN/OBDACHLOS/UN ANS-ABRI DU DOS ■

a vulnerability discovered, an intimacy revealed. While working, I engage in an unconscious process—advancing, suggesting, engaging, pulling back, whispering, courting silence, disappearing. Sometimes it works. □ Thumbing through periodicals today, it is often difficult to distinguish the work of one photographer from another. Style has become so overwhelming that often it overshadows content and the photographer's point of view. Style is imitable and easily adopted; photographs begin to look alike. For me, the heart guides the eye. If the camera describes, it is as descriptive of the photographer as it is of the subject. □ I look at my 5-year-old son and see his long, delicate lashes against transluscent skin. His face is young and fragile. I'm sad when I remember that he won't stay this way, and that were it not for the camera, my feelings for this moment would be forgotten. A photograph captures and protects; the photographer's heart guides the camera in recording the moment. □ Each photographer is unique. The distinction comes through in the work, so that a particular vision makes a body of work interesting, human and believable. The closer the camera is to the heart, and the more specific a vision becomes, the more successful the work. ■

MICHAEL O'BRIEN WAS BORN IN MEMPHIS, TENNESSEE, IN 1950. AFTER WORKING AS A NEWS PHOTOGRAPHER FOR THE *MIAMI NEWS*—HIS FIRST JOB—HE MOVED TO NEW YORK IN 1979. HIS CLIENTS INCLUDE *NATIONAL GEOGRAPHIC* MAGAZINE, *THE NEW YORK TIMES SUNDAY MAGAZINE*, *LIFE* MAGAZINE, NIKE, APPLE COMPUTER AND KODAK. MICHAEL O'BRIEN HAS WON TWO ROBERT F. KENNEDY JOURNALISM AWARDS; HIS WORK IS IN THE PERMANENT COLLECTIONS OF THE BIRMINGHAM MUSEUM OF ART AND THE INTERNATIONAL CENTER OF PHOTOGRAPHY IN NEW YORK.

Schon als kleiner Junge war ich ein Aussenseiter – statt mitzumachen, beobachtete und träumte ich lieber aus sicherer Entfernung. Es geht mir auch heute ähnlich: wenn ich anderen gegenübersitze, erinnere ich danach viel eher was ich gesehen und gefühlt, als was ich gehört habe: Ich sehe, wie das Licht auf ihre Gesichter fällt, wie die Jugendlichkeit der Gesichter dem Alter weicht, oder umgekehrt; wie sich bei den Worten der Gesichtsausdruck verändert, sehe ihre Stimmungen. Aber Bilder verblassen und mit ihnen jene Momente und Gefühle. Die Kamera jedoch kann festhalten, was die Zeit auslöscht. □ Schon immer habe ich gern Leute photographiert. Für mich ist das der Zweck einer Kamera. Die Photographie liess mich nicht mehr los, nachdem ich gemerkt hatte, dass ich mit der Kamera auf alle Leute, die mich interessierten, losgehen konnte. Vorher stand ich abseits und sah zu; mit meiner Kamera konnte ich teilnehmen. □ Meine Arbeit hat mir einen Zugang zu Leuten und Orten verschafft, die ich sonst nie kennengelernt hätte. Dank meiner Arbeit bereiste ich mein Land und die ganze Welt; ich photographierte einen australischen Viehzüchter, einen in einem Flussbett in Arizona lebenden Mann ebenso wie den Country-music Star Willie Nelson. □ Oft schauen meine Modelle in die Kamera – direkt und spontan. Es ist interessant – und wichtig – zu beobachten, wie sie die Kamera ansehen, wie ihre Augen das Objektiv suchen, und man muss sie gewähren lassen. Wenn ich in den Sucher schaue, merke ich, ob eine Verbindung besteht oder nicht. □ Oft spüre ich, wenn ich ein gutes Bild mache: Eine Verbindung ist entstanden, eine Verletzlichkeit entdeckt, etwas Wesentliches zum Vorschein gekommen. Wenn ich arbeite, gehe ich nach einem unbewussten Muster vor: Ich gehe aus mir heraus, mache Vorschläge, engagiere mich, ziehe mich zurück, flüstere, schweige, verschwinde. Manchmal funktioniert es. □ Wenn man heute Zeitschriften durchblättert, ist es oft schwer, zwischen den Arbeiten der verschiedenen Photographen zu unterscheiden. Stil ist so wichtig geworden, dass Inhalt und Standpunkt des Photographen kaum mehr erkennbar sind. Für mich führt die Seele das Auge. Wenn die Kamera beschreibt, beschreibt sie nicht allein das Modell, sondern auch den Photographen. □ Ich schaue meinen fünfjährigen Sohn an und sehe seine langen, seidigen Wimpern, die sich gegen die zarte Haut abheben. Sein Gesicht ist jung und unschuldig. Es stimmt mich traurig, daran zu denken, dass er sich verändern wird. Was ich in diesem Moment fühle, ginge verloren, gäbe es die Kamera nicht. Eine Photographie fängt ein und schützt; die Seele des Photographen lenkt die Kamera, die den Augenblick festhält. □ Jeder Photograph ist einzigartig. Seine Besonderheit zeigt sich in seiner Arbeit, sein Standpunkt macht seine Arbeit interessant, menschlich und glaubwürdig. □ Je näher die Kamera dem Herzen ist, um so spezieller werden die Bilder, um so erfolgreicher ist die Arbeit. ■

MICHAEL O'BRIEN WURDE 1950 IN MEMPHIS, TENNESSEE, GEBOREN. SEINEN ERSTEN JOB HATTE ER ALS BILDREPORTER FÜR *MIAMI NEWS*. 1979 MACHTE ER SICH IN NEW YORK SELBSTÄNDIG. ZU SEINEN AUFTRAGGEBERN GEHÖREN DAS MAGAZIN *NATIONAL GEOGRAPHIC, DAS NEW YORK TIMES SUNDAY MAGAZINE* UND *LIFE* SOWIE IM WERBEBEREICH NIKE, APPLE COMPUTER, KODAK UND WRANGLER JEANS. ER BEKAM ZWEI ROBERT-F.-KENNEDY AUSZEICHNUNGEN IM BEREICH DES PHOTOJOURNALISMUS, UND ER IST MIT SEINEN ARBEITEN IN DEN SAMMLUNGEN DES BIRMINGTON MUSEUM OF ART UND DES INTERNATIONAL CENTER OF PHOTOGRAPHY IN NEW YORK VERTRETEN.

Depuis mon enfance, j'ai toujours été un outsider – préférant observer, rêver à distance, plutôt que participer. Aujourd'hui encore, lorsque je suis assis en train de discuter avec d'autres personnes dans une pièce, je me rappelle plus distinctement ce que j'ai vu et senti que ce que j'ai entendu; comment la lumière tombait sur un visage, révélant les atteintes de l'âge, ou le contraire; comment les expressions des visages peuvent changer avec les mots, ainsi que les humeurs. Mais les images s'évanouissent et je me désole quand je réalise que ces instants et les sentiments qu'ils suscitaient sont passés. Seul l'appareil photo préserve ce que le temps efface. □ J'ai toujours eu envie de photographier des gens. Pour moi, c'est le rôle même de l'appareil photo. Dès le début, quand je l'ai utilisé pour approcher quelqu'un d'intimidant qui m'intriguait, j'étais fasciné. Avant que je ne me lance dans la photographie, je restais à la périphérie des choses, observant; avec mon appareil, je peux désormais participer. □ Mon activité m'a permis de découvrir des gens et des endroits que je n'aurais jamais connus autrement. Ma vocation m'a entraîné au travers de tout le pays et dans le monde entier: j'ai aussi bien photographié un gardien de bestiaux australien qu'un sans-logis de l'Arizona, ou encore la star de la country music Willie Nelson. □ Souvent, mes sujets fixent spontanément l'appareil photo. Il est intéressant – et essentiel – de voir comment leurs yeux rencontrent l'objectif, chacun à sa manière. En me concentrant sur le viseur, je peux ressentir la relation, ou l'absence de relation. □ Quand je fais une bonne photo, je m'en rends souvent compte: une relation s'établit, une vulnérabilité est mise à jour, une intimité révélée. Tout en travaillant, je m'engage dans un processus inconscient – je sors de moi-même, je fais des suggestions, je m'engage, ou au contraire, je me retire, murmure, deviens silencieux, ou bien je disparais. Parfois ça marche. □ En feuilletant des périodiques aujourd'hui, il est souvent difficile de distinguer l'œuvre d'un photographe de celle d'un autre. Le style prédomine tellement que la plupart du temps, il éclipse le contenu et le point de vue du photographe. Un style peut être imité et facilement adopté; les photographies commencent à toutes se ressembler. □ Pour moi, le cœur guide l'œil. Si l'appareil photo a un rôle descriptif, il décrit autant le photographe que son sujet. □ Je regarde mon fils de cinq ans et je vois ses longues mèches délicates se détacher sur sa peau translucide. Son visage est jeune et fragile. Je suis triste de penser qu'il n'en sera pas toujours ainsi et que, s'ils ne sont pas fixés par l'appareil photo, mes sentiments de cet instant seront oubliés. Une photographie capture et protège; le cœur du photographe guide l'appareil, permettant de fixer un moment privilégié. Chaque photographe est unique. Son originalité se manifeste dans son travail, c'est sa vision particulière qui rend son travail intéressant, humain et crédible. Plus l'appareil est proche du cœur, plus la vision est spécifique, et plus la photo est réussie. ■

MICHAEL O'BRIEN EST NÉ À MEMPHIS, TENNESSEE, EN 1950. APRÉS AVOIR ÉTÉ PHOTOGRAPHE DU JOURNAL *MIAMI NEWS* – IL PARTIT TRAVAILLER EN FREE-LANCE À NEW YORK. PARMI SES CLIENTS DANS LE SECTEUR ÉDITORIAL, ON TROUVE LE *NATIONAL GEOGRAPHIC*, *LE NEW YORK TIMES SUNDAY MAGAZINE* ET *LIFE*; IL A RÉALISÉ DES PUBLICITÉS POUR NIKE, APPLE COMPUTER, KODAK ET WRANGLER JEANS. IL A REMPORTÉ DEUX FOIS LE PRIX ROBERT F. KENNEDY, CATÉGORIE JOURNALISME; SES PHOTOS FIGURENT DANS LA COLLECTION PERMANENTE DU BIRMINGHAM MUSEUM OF ART ET DU INTERNATIONAL CENTER OF PHOTOGRAPHY À NEW YORK.

NOB FUKUDA

We can divide photography into two categories. One is the documentary: "taking photos," just for accurate illustration or records. The other is the creative: "making photos," which implies a concept on the part of the photographer. I work in the latter category. □ One doesn't need to "make" photos to report news or information. But you need to "make" photos in my field: advertising. It is my goal as a photographer to make people interested, to inspire them and to make them react in ways that only photography can bring about. □ Recently it became very easy to retouch, compose or change an image by computer. But one can't impress people with technique and gimmicks. I wish to do something that the computer cannot do. I wish to try something that nobody else has done. The photos shown here carry my message: the relationship of a "made" image and a "taken" image. I have done some handwork on these photos. My images have themes like: "Canvas," "Old Table," "Cubic Object Made With Iron Wire." They are all "made" images, but they could be "taken" images. □ I have tried to make you feel the passage of time, mixing virtual and real. I trust that we can take a new approach to advertising if its creators give some thought to my method as a photographer. If you cannot impress people, if you cannot take their breath away, the work is already outdated. ■

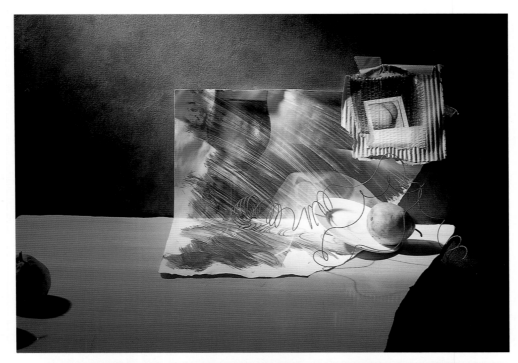

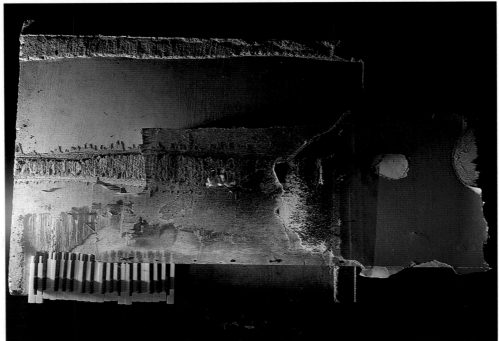

NOB FUKUDA WAS BORN IN OSAKA IN 1939. AFTER FINISHING HIS STUDIES AT THE OSAKA SCHOOL OF PROFESSIO-NAL PHOTOGRAPHY HE STUDIED THE ART OF PHOTO TECHNIQUE UNDER ONE OF JAPAN'S MOST RENOWNED MASTERS OF PHOTOGRAPHY, T. IWAMIYA. FUKUDA WORKS AS A FREELANCE PHOTOGRAPHER, SPECIALIZING IN STILL LIFES.

(OPPOSITE TOP) CLIENT: "PORTFOLIO" DESIGN MAGAZINE DESCRIPTION: A PHOTOGRAPH FOR AN EDITORIAL CATERGORY/AUFNAHME FÜR DEN REDAKTIONELLEN BEREICH/PHOTO DU SECTEUR ÉDITORIAL ■ (OPPOSITE BOTTOM) CLIENT: PONY CANION INC. ART DIRECTOR: YUSAKU NAKANISHI DESCRIPTION: RECORD JACKET FOR MAR-PA/SCHALLPLATTENHÜLLE FÜR MAR-PA/POCHETTE DE DISQUE POUR MAR-PA ■ (ABOVE) CLIENT: KAMITANI INC. ART DIRECTOR: TERUO TANAKA DESCRIPTION: ADVERTISING CALENDAR/WERBEKALENDER/CALENDRIER PUBLICITAIRE ■

Man kann die Photographie in zwei Kategorien teilen. Bei der einen geht es um das reine Dokumentieren, das Aufzeichnen von Gegebenheiten. Zur anderen gehört das kreative Konzipieren von Photos. □ Meine Photos gehören in diese zweite Kategorie. Um über die Tagesgeschehnisse zu informieren oder reine Informationen zu vermitteln, konzipiert man nicht. Die Realität ist für diese Photos ausschlaggebend. □ In der Werbebranche hingegen, für die ich arbeite, muss man Photos erdenken. Man muss sich eine Menge einfallen lassen. □ Ich sehe meine Aufgabe als Photograph darin, die Menschen für etwas zu interessieren, zu inspirieren, sie etwas spüren zu lassen, das man nur mit der Photographie ausdrücken kann. □ Heute begegnet man der Photographie nicht nur in der Werbung, auch Künstler machten die Photographie zu ihrem Medium. □ Durch reine Technik oder Spielereien gelingt es kaum, die Leute zu beeindrucken. Dank des Fortschritts in der Phototechnik ist es neuerdings sehr einfach geworden, jedes Bild mit Hilfe des Computers zu retuschieren, zu komponieren oder zu kombinieren. □ Ich möchte aber etwas machen, das der Computer nicht kann. Ich möchte Neues versuchen, was niemand zuvor gemacht hat. Wie ein Handwerker möchte ich künstlerisches und handwerkliches Können miteinander verbinden. □ Mir geht es um die Relation zwischen einem «eigentlichen» und einem «wirklichen» Bild. Die hier gezeigten Aufnahmen habe ich von Hand bearbeitet. Es sind «eigentliche» Bilder, könnten aber auch «wirkliche» Bilder sein. □ Ich kann nur ein Kunstwerk vollenden, indem ich entscheide, wie ich die real vorhandenen Eigenschaften komponiere und zu einem wirklichen Bild werden lasse. Ich habe versucht, die Dimension der Zeit einzubringen, indem ich das Eigentliche mit dem Wirklichen verbinde. □ Ich bin überzeugt, dass man auch in der Werbung neue Wege finden kann, wenn man in dieser Richtung arbeitet. □ Wenn es nicht gelingt, die Menschen zu beeindrucken, ihnen den Atem zu rauben, ist die Arbeit bereits vergessen und verloren. ■

NOB FUKUDA WURDE 1939 IN OSAKA GEBOREN. NACH ABSCHLUSS DER PHOTOSCHULE IN OSAKA LERNTE ER PHOTOTECHNIK BEI T. IWAMIYA, EINEM BERÜHMTEN MEISTER DES FACHS. FUKUDA HAT SICH AUF STILLLEBEN UND WERBEPHOTOGRAPHIE SPEZIALISIERT, MÖCHTE SICH ABER VERMEHRT. DER KÜNSTERISCHEN PHOTOGRAPHIE ZUWENDEN

On peut diviser la photographie en deux catégories. L'une se préoccupe uniquement de documenter, d'enregistrer des souvenirs. L'autre relève de la création. □ Je me range dans cette deuxième catégorie. On ne fait pas de la photo uniquement pour informer des événements de la journée ou pour transmettre une information. C'est la réalité qui détermine ce type de photos. □ Dans la publicité par contre, le domaine dans lequel je travaille, il est nécessaire de concevoir vraiment les photos. Il faut pour cela avoir beaucoup d'idées et de fantaisie. □ Ma tâche consiste à intéresser les gens à quelque chose, les inspirer, leur faire ressentir ce que l'on ne peut exprimer qu'au moyen de la photographie. □ Aujourd'hui, la photographie n'est pas exclusivement utilisée dans le seul secteur de la publicité, les artistes en ont fait également leur moyen d'expression. Ils savent inventer les idées les plus farfelues! □ Certes, il n'est pas possible d'impressionner les gens uniquement avec des astuces techniques ou des gags. Grâce aux progrès technologiques, il est devenu depuis quelque temps très simple de retoucher, de composer ou de combiner une image à l'aide de l'ordinateur. □ Mais j'aimerais faire ce que cet instrument ne fait pas. J'aimerais essayer quelque chose de nouveau, quelque chose que personne n'a jamais fait auparavant. J'aimerais, comme un artisan, associer la création artistique et le savoir-faire artisanal. □ Il en va pour moi de la relation entre une image «virtuelle» et une image «réelle» Dans les exemples présentés ici, j'ai retravaillé les photos à la main. Ce sont des images virtuelles, mais elles pourraient tout aussi bien être des images réelles. □ Je ne peux réaliser une œuvre d'art qu'en décidant comment composer les propriétés réelles disponibles et les transformer en une image véritable. Je m'efforce d'y ajouter une dimension temporelle en mélangeant le «virtuel» et le «réel». □ Je suis persuadé que l'on peut également explorer de nouvelles voies dans la publicité, si l'on travaille dans cette optique. Si vous ne réussissez pas à impressionner les gens, à leur couper le souffle, alors c'est que votre travail est déjà suranné. ∎

NOB FUKUDA EST NÉ À OSAKA EN 1939. APRÈS SES ÉTUDES À L'ÉCOLE DE PHOTOGRAPHIE, IL PERFECTIONNA SON APPRENTISSAGE DE LA TECHNIQUE AUPRÈS DE T. IWAMIYA, L'UN DES PLUS GRANDS MAÎTRES DE LA PHOTOGRAPHIE AU JAPON. DEPUIS LE DÉBUT DE SA CARRIÈRE, NOB FUKUDA TRAVAILLE EN FREE-LANCE. IL EST SPÉCIALISÉ DANS LA PHOTO PUBLICITAIRE ET LA NATURE MORTE. IL DÉSIRE SE CONCENTRER À L'AVENIR SUR LA PHOTOGRAPHIE D'ART.

AERNOUT OVERBEEKE

As a child, I loved to visit my grandparents. They lived in the center of Rotterdam in a narrow, top-floor apartment where they had brought up their nine children. Before reaching the living room you had to climb three steep, narrow sets of stairs. The house was small but very cosy. □ In the attic, where we grandchildren played, was a room where, years ago, my aunts and uncles had slept. But now that all the children had long since left the house, granddad had claimed this space to himself. He considered it his private domain and preferred us not to enter unaccompanied. □ In the room stood a chair, a table and an easel. A small vase stood on the table. There were brushes in the vase and next to it lay tubes of paint and a palette. An unfinished canvas was often on the easel. Looking at that canvas, wondering how it would look when finished, was probably the first time in my life that I found myself fascinated by an image caught on a flat surface. □ My grandfather didn't use his imagination when painting his pictures. He copied picture postcards, reproductions of paintings. Even though his copies were close to the originals, the results were always a little different. He put his soul into them. □ I thought it was very special that the man who made these paintings was my granddad. I was intensely proud of him. □ Later, when I went to high school, I often visited the

(ABOVE, ALL IMAGES) PERSONAL WORK FOR AN EXHIBITION ENTITLED "IN THE GARDEN OF EDEN"/FÜR EINE AUSSTELLUNG «IM GARTEN EDEN»/POUR UNE EXPOSITION INTITULÉE «AU JARDIN D'EDEN» ■ (OPPOSITE) CONSTRUCTION, SANS SOUCIS, BERLIN, 1991/BAU, SANS SOUCIS, BERLIN, 1991/BÂTIMENT, SANS SOUCIS, BERLIN, 1991 ■

Rijksmuseum and the Stedelijk Museum. I was astounded and amazed. It was wonderful to be surrounded by beautiful masterpieces. It was probably there that I really started looking. Looking, at first, without understanding what I saw. Feeling the emotion, but not knowing why. It takes years to understand why a certain image arouses a certain emotion. Much later still, one can hope to create images that will arouse emotions in other people. But that is very difficult to do. □ My grandfather was a collector of beautiful pictures and postcards. I am also a collector. Photography is like catching butterflies, setting them and placing them in a beautiful cabinet. To catch that short, wonderful moment that flutters by, to print it and to frame it. Before you know it they are no longer there, things of the past, gone, dead. Some butterflies live but one day. □ How difficult it is to catch butterflies! ■

AERNOUT OVERBEEKE WAS BORN IN THE NETHERLANDS, IN 1951. THE FIRST TEN YEARS OF HIS CAREER WERE MAINLY DEVOTED TO FASHION PHOTOGRAPHY. AT THE AGE OF 30 OVERBEEKE SWITCHED TO LANDSCAPE PHOTOGRAPHY. HIS EARLY RESULTS WERE SUCCESSFUL ENOUGH TO ENCOURAGE HIM TO CONTINUE. TODAY, AERNOUT OVERBEEKE WORKS FOR NUMEROUS INTERNATIONAL CLIENTS ON LOCATION IN ALL PARTS OF THE WORLD.

. . . .

Als Kind liebte ich es, meine Grosseltern zu besuchen. Sie lebten mitten in Rotterdam, in einer Wohnung ganz oben in einem schmalen Haus, in der sie ihre neun Kinder gross-gezogen hatten. Bevor man die Wohnräume erreichte, musste man drei steile, schmale Treppen hinaufsteigen. Das Haus war klein, aber sehr gemütlich. Unter dem Dach, wo wir Enkelkinder spielten, befand sich ein Raum, in dem vor Jahren meine Tanten und Onkel geschlafen hat-ten. Jetzt, nachdem alle Kinder längst das Haus verlassen hatten, wurde dieser Raum von meinem Grossvater für sich in Anspruch genommen. Er betrachtete ihn als sein ganz privates Reich, und wir durften nur hinein, wenn er dort war. □ In dem Raum stand ein Stuhl, ein Tisch und eine Staffelei. Auf dem Tisch befand sich eine kleine Vase. Es waren Pinsel darin, daneben lagen Farbtuben und eine Palette. Oft stand auf der Staffelei eine kleine, noch unfer-tige Leinwand. Ich betrachtete diese Leinwände und über-legte, wie das fertige Bild wohl aussehen würde. Wohl zum ersten Mal in meinem Leben war ich fasziniert von einem Bild auf einer flachen Oberfläche. □ Mein Grossvater malte nicht nach seiner eigenen Phantasie. Er kopierte Bildpostkarten, Reproduktionen bereits existierender Bilder. Obgleich seine Kopien den Originalen sehr ähnel-ten, war das Ergebnis doch immer ein bisschen anders. Er legte seine Seele in diese Bilder. □ Ich war sehr stolz darauf, den Mann, der diese Bilder malte, zu kennen, und noch stolzer war ich, dass er mein Grossvater war. Ich war unendlich stolz auf ihn. □ Später, als ich die höhere Schule besuchte, hatte ich das Glück, ganz nah beim Rijksmuse-um und dem Stedelijk Museum zu sein – beide waren nur einen Steinwurf weit von der Schule entfernt. Ich besuchte diese Museen häufig. Ich war vollkommen überwältigt und fühlte mich grossartig inmitten all der wunderbaren Meisterwerke. Ich glaube, in jener Zeit lernte ich zu schauen. Zuerst schaut man ohne zu verstehen, was man sieht. Man spürt etwas, weiss aber nicht warum. Später – ich brauchte Jahre – lernt man zu verstehen, warum ein bestimmtes Bild ein bestimmtes Gefühl weckt. Noch viel später hofft man, selbst Bilder zu machen, die bei anderen Menschen bestimmte Gefühle hervorrufen. Aber das ist sehr schwer. □ Mein Grossvater war ein Sammler schöner Bilder. Er kaufte eine schöne Postkarte und kopierte sie. □ Auch ich bin Sammler. Photographieren ist wie das Fangen von Schmetterlingen, man konserviert sie und stellt sie in einer schönen Vitrine aus. Man fängt einen kurzen, wunderbaren Moment ein, der an einem vorbei-flattert, das Bild wird gedruckt und eingerahmt. Bevor man sich versieht, sind sie nicht mehr da, vergangen, vorbei, tot. Einige Schmetterlinge leben nur einen Tag lang. □ Es ist schwer, Schmetterlinge zu fangen! ■

AERNOUT OVERBEEKE WURDE 1951 IN UTRECHT GEBOREN. NACH DER SCHULE MACHTE ER EINE LEHRE IN EINEM PHOTOSTUDIO, UND IM ALTER VON 20 ERHIELT ER SEINEN ERSTEN AUFTRAG. ZEHN JAHRE LANG BEFASSTE ER SICH VOR ALLEM MIT MODEAUFNAHMEN. SCHLIESSLICH SEHNTE ER SICH NACH ETWAS ANDEREM UND MACHTE SEINE ERSTEN VERSUCHE IN DER LANDSCHAFTSPHOTOGRAPHIE. ER HATTE GERADE SOVIEL ERFOLG, UM NICHT DEN MUT ZU VERLIEREN. SCHLIESSLICH GAB ER DIE MODEPHOTOGRAPHIE AUF UND BEMÜHTE SICH UM AUFTRÄGE, DIE MEHR MIT SEINER FREIEN ARBEIT ZU TUN HATTEN. HEUTE ARBEITET ER FÜR AUFTRAGGEBER IN DER GANZEN WELT.

Enfant, j'adorais aller en visite chez mes grands-parents. Ils habitaient au cœur de Rotterdam, dans un étroit appartement situé au dernier étage, où ils avaient élevé leurs neuf enfants. Pour entrer au salon, il fallait d'abord grimper trois escaliers étroits et raides. Leur maison était petite, mais ô combien chaleureuse. □ Au grenier où, petits-enfants, nous allions jouer, se trouvait une chambre qui, il y a bien des années de cela, avait servi de chambre à coucher à mes oncles et tantes. Mais une fois tous les enfants envolés du nid familial, grand-père s'était attribué cet espace. C'était son domaine à lui et il préférait ne pas nous y voir entrer seuls. □ La pièce comportait une chaise, une table et un chevalet. Sur la table, un splendide petit vase. Dans ce vase se trouvaient des pinceaux et à côté, des tubes de couleurs et une palette. La plupart du temps, le chevalet supportait une petite toile non terminée. Je fixais cette toile, me demandant à quoi cela ressemblerait une fois terminé; cette expérience a sans doute marqué ma première fascination pour l'image encadrée, réalisée sur une surface plane. □ Mon grand-père ne faisait jamais appel à sa propre fantaisie pour peindre ses tableaux. Il copiait des cartes postales, reproductions de tableaux existants. Bien que ses copies fussent proches de l'original, le résultat final s'en distinguait toujours un peu. Cette petite différence, c'était la part d'âme qu'il y avait investi. □ Je considérais comme un honneur spécial de pouvoir connaître l'homme qui réalisait ces tableaux; mais surtout le fait que cet homme était mon grand-père. J'étais profondément fier de lui. □ Plus tard, au lycée, j'ai eu la chance de me retrouver dans une situation particulièrement favorable. Je pouvais en effet me rendre au Rijksmuseum et au Stedelijk Museum aussi souvent que je voulais. Et j'y allai souvent. Entouré de ces chefs-d'œuvres magnifiques, l'étonnement, la stupeur et l'immense joie de me retrouver ici me comblaient. C'est d'ailleurs probablement dans ces musées que j'ai commencé à vraiment savoir regarder. Regarder, oui, sans comprendre ce que l'on voit. Eprouver une émotion, mais ne pas savoir pourquoi. Plus tard – cela m'a pris des années – on apprend à comprendre pourquoi telle image suscite telle émotion. Et beaucoup plus tard encore, on espère soi-même réussir à créer des images capables de susciter des émotions semblables chez d'autres personnes. Mais cela est très difficile. Mon grand-père collectionnait de beaux tableaux. Il achetait une belle carte postale, puis il la copiait. □ Moi aussi, je suis devenu collectionneur. Photographier, c'est comme chasser des papillons, les préparer et les placer dans une belle vitrine. Parvenir à saisir ce bref instant merveilleux qui volète devant vous, l'imprimer ensuite, enfin l'encadrer. Car avant de s'en apercevoir, ils ont disparu, appartenant déjà au passé, partis, morts. Certains papillons ne vivent qu'un seul jour, savez-vous! Attraper des papillons, c'est difficile! ■

AERNOUT OVERBEEKE EST NÉ À UTRECHT EN 1951. APRÈS AVOIR TERMINÉ SES ÉTUDES, IL ENTRA EN APPRENTISSAGE CHEZ UN PHOTOGRAPHE, ET À L'ÂGE DE 20 ANS, IL RECEVAIT SA PREMIÈRE COMMANDE. DIX ANS PLUS TARD, IL FAISAIT PRESQUE EXCLUSIVEMENT DE LA PHOTO DE MODE. PLUS TARD, DÉSIREUX DE FAIRE DE NOUVELLES EXPÉRIENCES, IL COMMENÇA À PHOTOGRAPHIER DES PAYSAGES. IL EUT JUSTE ASSEZ DE SUCCÈS POUR NE PAS SE DÉCOURAGER. FINALEMENT, IL ABANDONNA LA PHOTOGRAPHIE DE MODE ET SE PRÉOCCUPA DE TROUVER DES COMMANDES EN RAPPORT AVEC SES ÉTUDES LIBRES. AUJOURD'HUI, IL TRAVAILLE POUR DES CLIENTS DU MONDE ENTIER.

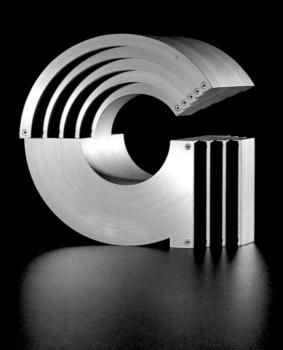

BEST FASHION (SERIES)

PHOTOGRAPHER: GOTTFRIED HELNWEIN

CLIENT: KATHLEEN MADDEN

BEST STILL LIFE

PHOTOGRAPHER: JONATHAN LOVEKIN

PERSONAL WORK

BEST FOOD

PHOTOGRAPHER: ROSANNE OLSON

SELF PROMOTION

BEST PEOPLE

PHOTOGRAPHER: HERB RITTS

PERSONAL WORK

BEST OUTDOOR

PHOTOGRAPHER: PETE STONE

SELF PROMOTION

BEST PRODUCT

PHOTOGRAPHER: MICHAEL NORTHRUP

CLIENT: THE GALLERY OF MARKET EAST MALL

AWARD SCULPTURE "G" FROM THE ALUMINUM ALPHABET BY TAKENOBU IGARASHI

FASHION

MODE

MODE

■ 1 (FIRST PAGE OF FASHION SECTION) POR-
TRAIT OF RINA KASTRELLI FOR A CATALOG OF
SPANISH FASHION DESIGNER SYBILLA. IT HAS
ALSO BEEN USED IN A CATALOG OF PARIS
MODEL AGENCY FAM. (SPA)

■ 2-5 PHOTOGRAPHS TAKEN ON LOCATION
AND IN THE STUDIO FOR THE GUESS?, INC.
FOOTWEAR CATALOG. (USA)

● 1 (ERSTE SEITE) PORTRÄT VON RINA
KASTRELLI FÜR EINEN MODEKATALOG VON
SYBILLA. DIE AUFNAHME WURDE AUSSERDEM
IN EINEM KATALOG DER MODELLAGENTUR FAM
GEZEIGT. (SPA)

● 2-5 AUFNAHMEN FÜR EINEN SCHUHKATALOG.
SIE WURDEN MIT EINER 4X5" KAMERA IM
STUDIO UND AUSSERHALB GEMACHT. (USA)

▲ 1 (PREMIÉRE PAGE) PHOTO DE NINA
KASTRELLI RÉALISÉE POUR LE CATALOGUE DE
MODE DE SYBILLA ET PUBLIÉE DANS LE CATA-
LOGUE DE MODÈLES DE L'AGENCE FAM, À
PARIS. (SPA)

▲ 2-5 PHOTOS ILLUSTRANT UN CATALOGUE DE
CHAUSSURES. ELLES ONT ÉTÉ PRISES EN
STUDIO ET À L'EXTÉRIEUR. (USA)

(FIRST PAGE OF
FASHION SECTION)
PHOTOGRAPHER:
JAVIER VALLHONRAT
REPRESENTATIVE:
MICHELE FILOMENO
CLIENTS:
SYBILLA,
AGENCE FAM/
FABIENNE MARTIN

ART DIRECTORS:
JUAN GATTI,
BENITA RAPHAN
DESIGNER:
SYBILLA,
BENITA RAPHAN
STUDIO:
MICHELE FILOMENO
1

PHOTOGRAPHERS:
LOISE O'BRIEN,
DANIEL SCHRIDDE
CLIENT:
GUESS?, INC.
ART DIRECTOR:
PAUL MARCIANO
DESIGNER:
SAMANTHA GIBSON
AGENCY:
GUESS?, INC.
IN-HOUSE
2-5

PHOTOGRAPHER:

HERB RITTS

REPRESENTATIVE:

VISAGES

CLIENT:

AGENCE FAM,

FABIENNE MARTIN

ART DIRECTOR:

BENITA RAPHAN

DESIGNER:

BENITA RAPHAN

AGENCY:

BENITA RAPHAN

DESIGN

< 6

PHOTOGRAPHER:

JAVIER VALLHONRAT

REPRESENTATIVE:

MICHELE FILOMENO

CLIENT:

JIL SANDER

ART DIRECTOR:

MARC ASCOLI

DESIGNER:

BENITA RAPHAN

AGENCY:

MARC ASCOLI

STUDIO:

MICHELE FILOMENO

7

■ 6 THIS PHOTOGRAPH BY HERB RITTS OF NASTASIA URBANO WAS ORGINALLY PUBLISHED IN *PICTURES*. IT WAS REPUBLISHED AS PART OF AN OVERVIEW OF FASHION PHOTOGRAPHY BY THE FAM MODEL AGENCY. (FRA)

■ 7 THIS PHOTOGRAPH WAS USED IN A CATALOG FOR GERMAN FASHION DESIGNER JIL SANDER. (GER)

● 6 HERB RITTS' PORTRÄT VON NASTASIA URBANO WURDE URSPRÜNGLICH IN DEM BUCH *PICTURES* VERÖFFENTLICHT. ES WURDE DANACH IN EINEM KATALOG DER FAM MODELLAGENTUR VERWENDET. (FRA)

● 7 DIESE AUFNAHME WURDE FÜR EINEN KATALOG VON DER DEUTSCHEN MODE-DESIGNERIN JIL SANDER VERWENDET. (GER)

▲ 6 CE PORTRAIT DE NASTASIA URBANO PAR HERB RITTS, REPRODUITE DANS LE CATALOGUE DE L'AGENCE DE MODÉLES PARISIENNE FAM, A ÉTÉ PUBLIÉE DANS LE LIVRE *PICTURES*. (FRA)

▲ 7 CETTE PHOTO A ÉTÉ REPRODUITE DANS UN CATALOGUE JIL SANDER, POUR UNE MODE CLASSIQUE. (GER)

PHOTOGRAPHER:
HANS HANSEN
CLIENT:
MUSTANG
BEKLEIDUNGSWERKE
ART DIRECTOR:
PETRA HOCK
STYLIST:
GERTRUDIS WEISNER
AGENCY:
LEONHARDT & KERN
8, 9

PHOTOGRAPHER:
SERGEJ KISCHNICK
CAMERA:
SINAR P 4X5"
FILM:
POLAROID P/N55
CLIENT:
AUGOSTINO NORI
ART DIRECTOR:
SERGEJ KISCHNICK
DESIGNER:
SERGEJ KISCHNICK
> 10

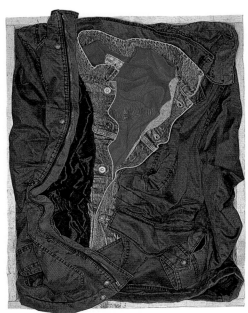

■ 8, 9 THESE PHOTOGRAPHS WERE TAKEN FOR A CATALOG PRESENTING MUSTANG MODERN CLASSIC APPAREL. (GER)

■ 10 PORTRAIT FROM A BLACK-AND-WHITE SERIES FOR THE 1990 FASHION COLLECTION OF AUGOSTINO NORI. THE DISCUSSION ON THE FASCINATING COLLECTION WENT ON FOR HOURS SO THAT THE PHOTOGRAPHER ALMOST FORGOT ABOUT WORK. HE WAS LEFT WITH 15 MINUTES TO SHOOT FOUR PHOTOGRAPHS (4X5" ON POLAROID P/N 55). (ITA)

● 8, 9 DIESE AUFNAHMEN STAMMEN AUS EINEM KATALOG FÜR MODE DER MARKE MUSTANG MODERN CLASSIC. (GER)

● 10 AUS EINER SERIE IN SCHWARZWEISS FÜR DIE KOLLEKTION 1990 DES MODEDESIGNERS AUGOSTINO NORI. DIE KOLLEKTION WAR SO FASZINIEREND, DASS ÜBER DIE GESPRÄCHE FAST DER PHOTOTERMIN VERGESSEN WURDE: DEM PHOTOGRAPHEN BLIEBEN GANZE 15 MINUTEN FÜR VIER AUFNAHMEN (4X5" AUF POLAROID P/N55). (ITA)

▲ 8, 9 PHOTOS TIRÉES D'UN CATALOGUE PRÉSENTANT LES MODÈLES DE LA COLLECTION MUSTANG MODERN CLASSIC. (GER)

▲ 10 PORTRAIT D'UNE SÉRIE EN NOIR ET BLANC POUR LA COLLECTION 1990 DU COUTURIER AUGOSTINO NORI. PLONGÉ DANS UNE DISCUSSION PASSIONNANTE À CE SUJET, LE PHOTOGRAPHE EN OUBLIA PRESQUE L'HEURE FIXÉE POUR LES PHOTOS: IL NE LUI RESTAIT PLUS QUE 15 MINUTES POUR RÉALISER QUATRE CLICHÉS. (ITA)

PHOTOGRAPHER: DESIGNER:

STEVEN MEISEL   REAL ART

REPRESENTATIVE: STYLIST:

ART + COMMERCE   NICOLETTA SANTORO

CLIENT: AGENCY:

ANTONIO FUSCO   SONCINI & GINEPRO

ART DIRECTOR: 11, 12

FRANCA SONCINI

■ 11, 12 TWO PHOTOGRAPHS FROM A LARGE-FORMAT CATALOG PRESENTING FASHION BY ITALIAN DESIGNER ANTONIO FUSCO. THE FULL-PAGE PHOTOGRAPHS ARE THE MAIN ELEMENTS IN THIS CATALOG. (ITA)

● 11, 12 ZWEI DER AUFNAHMEN AUS EINEM GROSSFORMATIGEN KATALOG FÜR ITALIENISCHE MODE VON ANTONIO FUSCO. DIE GANZSEITIGEN AUFNAHMEN SIND DAS DOMINIERENDE ELEMENT DIESES KATALOGS. (ITA)

▲ 11, 12 DEUX PHOTOS TIRÉES D'UN CATALOGUE GRAND FORMAT PRÉSENTANT LES CRÉATIONS DU COUTURIER ITALIEN ANTONIO FUSCO. LES PHOTOS PLEINE PAGE CONSTITUENT L'ÉLÉMENT DOMINANT. (ITA)

PHOTOGRAPHER:
SUE BENNETT
CAMERA:
NIKON
FILM:
FUJI NEOPAN
13, 14

PHOTOGRAPHER:
ULRICH PRACHT
CAMERA:
NIKON F2
FILM:
EPR 64
CLIENT:
CAREN PFLEGER
DESIGN GMBH

ART DIRECTOR:
STAN KAINZLER
DESIGNER:
CAREN PFLEGER
STUDIO:
ULRICH PRACHT
> 15

■ **13, 14** THESE PHOTOGRAPHS WERE TAKEN AS A TEST ON AN ABANDONED SHEEP RANCH IN ARIZONA. (USA)

■ **15** THE ASSIGNMENT BY FASHION DESIGNER, CAREN PFLEGER, FOR THIS PHOTOGRAPH WAS TO CREATE AN ATMOSPHERE EVOKING SENSATION AND DESIRE RATHER THAN PRESENTING JUST THE FASHION ITSELF. (GER)

● **13, 14** DIESE AUFNAHMEN WURDEN ALS TEST AUF EINER VERLASSENEN SCHAF-RANCH IN ARIZONA GEMACHT. (USA)

● **15** DER AUFTRAG FÜR DIESE AUFNAHME LAUTETE, NICHT DAS PRODUKT (MODE VON CAREN PFLEGER), SONDERN EINE SPEZIELLE ATMOSPHÄRE ZU SCHAFFEN, DIE SEHNSÜCHTE UND GEFÜHLE WECKT. (GER)

▲ **13, 14** CES PHOTOS, QUI SERVAIENT DE TEST, ONT ÉTÉ RÉALISÉES DANS UN RANCH ABANDONNÉ DE L'ARIZONA. (USA)

▲ **15** LA COMMANDE STIPULAIT DE NE PAS MONTRER UNIQUEMENT LE PRODUIT (LA MODE CAREN PFLEGER), MAIS DE CRÉER UNE ATMOSPHÈRE SUSCEPTIBLE D'ÉVEILLER LES SENTIMENTS ET LES SENSATIONS. (GER)

BEST FASHION (SERIES)
THIS SPREAD AND
FOLLOWING SPREAD
PHOTOGRAPHER:
GOTTFRIED HELNWEIN
ART DIRECTOR:
GOTTFRIED HELNWEIN
CLIENT:
KATHLEEN MADDEN
16-19

■ 16-19 (THIS SPREAD AND FOLLOWING SPREAD) PHOTOGRAPHS FROM A LARGE-FORMAT FASHION CATALOG FOR KATHLEEN MADDEN. PHOTOGRAPHER GOTTFRIED HELNWEIN, WHO IS ALSO A WELL-KNOWN PAINTER, WAS GIVEN FREE REIGN. THE SHOOTING TOOK PLACE IN POTSDAM, IN THE HOMES OF WORKING CLASS PEOPLE AND MEMBERS OF THE SOVIET ARMY, AS WELL AS IN THE ARMY'S CLUBHOUSE. (GER)

● 16-19 (DIESE UND DIE FOLGENDE DOPPELSEITE) AUFNAHMEN AUS EINEM GROSSFORMATIGEN KATALOG FÜR MODE VON KATHLEEN MADDEN. DEM AUCH ALS MALER BEKANNTEN PHOTOGRAPHEN GOTTFRIED HELNWEIN WURDE VÖLLIG FREIE HAND GELASSEN. ER PHOTOGRAPHIERTE IN POTSDAM, VOR ALLEM IN WOHNUNGEN DER ARBEITERKLASSE UND DER SOWJETISCHEN SOLDATEN SOWIE IN DEREN CLUB. (GER)

▲ 16-19 (CETTE DOUBLE PAGE ET DOUBLE PAGE SUIVANTE) D'UN CATALOGUE GRAND FORMAT PRÉSENTANT LA COLLECTION DE MODE DE KATHLEEN MADDEN. LE PHOTOGRAPHE GOTTFRIED HELNWEIN, CONNU POUR SES PEINTURES HYPERRÉALISTES, AVAIT REÇU CARTE BLANCHE. LES PHOTOS ONT ÉTÉ PRISES À POTSDAM, DANS DES APPARTEMENTS ET AU CLUB DES SOLDATS SOVIÉTIQUES. (GER)

BEST FASHION (SERIES)
(CONTINUED THIS
SPREAD)
PHOTOGRAPHER:
GOTTFRIED HELNWEIN
ART DIRECTOR:
GOTTFRIED HELNWEIN
CLIENT:
KATHLEEN MADDEN
16-19

(FOLLOWING
SPREAD, LEFT PAGE)
PHOTOGRAPHER:
JAVIER VALLHONRAT
REPRESENTATIVE:
MICHELE FILOMENO
CLIENTS:
MARTINE SITBON,
AGENCE FAM/
FABIENNE MARTIN

ART DIRECTORS:
MARC ASCOLI,
BENITA RAPHAN
DESIGNERS:
MARTINE SITBON,
BENITA RAPHAN
CLIENT:
MARTINE SITBON
STUDIO:
MICHELE FILOMENO
> 20

(FOLLOWING
SPREAD, RIGHT PAGE)
PHOTOGRAPHER:
STEVEN KLEIN
REPRESENTATIVE:
MAREK & ASSOC.
CLIENT:
AGENCE FAM/
FABIENNE MARTIN

ART DIRECTOR:
BENITA RAPHAN
DESIGNER:
BENITA RAPHAN
AGENCY:
BENITA RAPHAN
DESIGN
> 21

■ 20 (FOLLOWING SPREAD, LEFT PAGE) THIS PORTRAIT OF ANA-MARINA KREGEL, ORGINALLY ASSIGNED FOR A CAMPAIGN BY FASHION DESIGNER MARTINE SITBON, WAS SUBSEQUENTLY USED IN A CATALOG OF THE FAM MODEL AGENCY. (FRA)

■ 21 (FOLLOWING SPREAD, RIGHT PAGE) THIS PORTRAIT OF GABRIELLE REECE WAS ORIGINALLY PUBLISHED IN A FASHION FEATURE OF BRITISH VOGUE. IT WAS ALSO USED IN A CATALOG OF THE FAM MODEL AGENCY. (GBR)

● 20 (FOLGENDE DOPPELSEITE LINKS) DIESES PORTRÄT VON ANA-MARINA KREGEL, URSPRÜNGLICH FÜR EINE KAMPAGNE DER MODEDESIGNERIN MARTINE SITBON GEMACHT, WURDE AUCH IN EINEM KATALOG DER FAM-MODELLAGENTUR VERWENDET. (FRA)

● 21 (FOLGENDE DOPPELSEITE RECHTS) AUFNAHME DES MODELLS GABRIELLE REECE AUS EINEM MODEBEITRAG IN DER BRITISCHEN VOGUE. SIE ERSCHIEN AUSSERDEM IN EINEM KATALOG DER MODELLAGENTUR FAM. (GBR)

▲ 20 (DOUBLE PAGE SUIVANTE À G.) PORTRAIT D'ANA-MARINA KREGEL RÉALISÉE POUR UNE CAMPAGNE D'ANNONCE DE LA CRÉATRICE DE MODE MARTIN SITBON ET REPRODUITE DANS LE CATALOGUE DE L'AGENCE DE MODÈLES FAM. (FRA)

▲ 21 (DOUBLE PAGE SUIVANTE À DR.) CETTE PHOTOGRAPHIE DE GABRIELLE REECE, A ÉTÉ PUBLIÉE DANS L'ÉDITION ANGLAISE DE VOGUE ET REPRODUITE DANS LE CATALOGUE DE L'AGENCE DE MODÈLES FAM, À PARIS. (GBR)

PHOTOGRAPHER:

IVO VON RENNER

CAMERA:

POLAROID SX 70

FILM:

POLAROID SX 70

22

PHOTOGRAPHER:

KERSTIN STELTER

CAMERA:

HASSELBLAD 150MM

FILM:

KODAK T-MAX 100

STYLISTS:

BEA GOSSMANN,

SUSANNE WEISS

> 23

■ 22 A DOUBLE POLAROID (SX 70 CAMERA WITH NIKON SB 24 FLASHLIGHT) FROM A SELF-ASSIGNED SERIES ENTITLED "TO OUR HEROINE, THE WOMAN COSMONAUT." AFTER HER RETURN TO EARTH THE LADY TAKES A VACATION ON THE ISLAND OF RÜGEN. (GER)

■ 23 THIS PHOTOGRAPH IS PART OF A FREE SERIES OF FASHION PHOTOS, WHICH HAD TO INTERPRET THE FLAIR OF DESIGNER FASHION AND AT THE SAME TIME OFFER A REALISTIC IMAGE OF THE APPAREL (COAT BY DOLCE & GABBANA). (GER)

● 22 DOPPELPOLAROID-AUFNAHME (MIT SX 70 KAMERA UND NIKONBLITZ 24 SB) AUS EINER FREIEN SERIE MIT DEM TITEL «UNSERER HELDIN, DER KOSMONAUTIN». NACH ERFOLG-REICHER RÜCKKEHR ZUR ERDE MACHT SIE FERIEN AUF DER INSEL RÜGEN. (GER)

● 23 DIESE AUFNAHME GEHÖRT ZU EINER FREIEN MODESERIE, IN DER ES UM DAS MIT DESIGNERMODE VERBUNDENE FLAIR UND DIE REALISTISCHE DARSTELLUNG DES KLEI-DUNGSSTÜCKES (MANTEL VON DOLCE & GABBANA) GEHT. (USA)

▲ 22 POLAROÏD DOUBLE (APPAREIL SX 70 AVEC FLASH NIKON 24 SB) D'UNE SÉRIE D'ÉTUDES INTITULÉE «NOTRE HÉROÏNE, LA COSMONAUTE». AU RETOUR D'UN VOL INTER-PLANÉTAIRE, LA COSMONAUTE RUSSE PASSA DES VACANCES SUR L'ÎLE DE RÜGEN. (GER)

▲ 23 PHOTO D'UNE SÉRIE D'ÉTUDES PERSON-NELLES SUR LA MODE. LA PHOTOGRAPHE A CHERCHÉ À INTERPRÉTER LES CRÉATIONS DES DESIGNERS ET À REPRÉSENTER LES VÊTEMENTS DE MANIÈRE RÉALISTE (MANTEAU DE DOLCE & GABBANA). (GER)

PHOTOGRAPHER:

H. ROSS FELTUS

CAMERA:

CANON

FILM:

KODAK PXP

CLIENT:

TROTINETTE

DESIGNER:

H. ROSS FELTUS

COLORATION:

ULRIKA RUDOLPH

< 24

PHOTOGRAPHER:

H. ROSS FELTUS

CAMERA:

CANON

FILM:

KODAK PXP

CLIENT:

ORELL FÜSSLI

WERBE AG

ART DIRECTOR:

THOMAS KREBS

HANDCOLORATION:

DORIS BALLMANN-

TSANGARIS

AGENCY:

MARTI, OGILVY

+ MATHER

25, 26

■ 24 THE SUBJECT OF THIS HAND-TINTED PHOTOGRAPH FOR FRENCH CHILDREN'S APPAREL MANUFACTURER, TROTINETTE, CONTRASTS JAPAN'S RIGIDITY IN HANDLING THINGS AGAINST THE MORE LIGHT-HEARTED EUROPEAN MENTALITY, E.G. WITH REGARD TO RELIGION. THIS PHOTOGRAPH REFERS TO EUROPEAN RELIGIONS THAT SET FOOT IN JAPAN. THE INTERPRETATION IS FULL OF HUMOR, JUST LIKE TROTINETTE'S STYLE WHICH IS ANYTHING BUT SEVERE. (FRA)

■ 25, 26 HAND-TINTED PHOTOGRAPHS PRINTED ON ILFORD GALERIE MATT STOCK FOR AN ORELL FÜSSLI IMAGE CAMPAIGN, PUBLISHERS OF MAGAZINES AND BOOKS. (SWI)

● 24 DAS THEMA DIESER HANDKOLORIERTEN AUFNAHME FÜR DEN KINDERMODEHERSTELLER TROTINETTE IST DER KONTRAST ZWISCHEN DER RIGOROSITÄT JAPANS IN ALLEN DINGEN UND DER UNBESCHWERTEREN MENTALITÄT DER EUROPÄER, Z.B. BEIM UMGANG MIT DER RELIGION. DIE AUFNAHME BEZIEHT SICH AUF DIE EUROPÄISCHEN RELIGIONEN, DIE AUCH IN JAPAN FUSS GEFASST HABEN. DIESE INTERPRETATION IST VOLLER HUMOR, WIE DIE MODE VON TROTINETTE. (FRA)

● 25, 26 HANDKOLORIERTE AUFNAHMEN, AUF ILFORD GALERIE MATT, FÜR EINE IMAGE-KAMPAGNE DER ORELL FÜSSLI UND IHRE ZEITSCHRIFTEN *WIR ELTERN* UND *ORELLA*. (SWI)

▲ 24 PHOTO COLORÉE MAIN POUR LA MARQUE FRANÇAISE DE VÊTEMENTS POUR ENFANTS, TROTINETTE. ELLE A POUR SUJET LE CONTRASTE ENTRE L'ESPRIT RIGOUREUX DES JAPONAIS ET CELUI, PLUS LÉGER, DES EUROPÉENS, ILLUSTRÉ ICI PAR L'ATTITUDE FACE AUX RELIGIONS: LA PHOTO FAIT ALLUSION AUX RELIGIONS EUROPÉENNES, QUI SE SONT IMPLANTÉES AU JAPON; CETTE INTERPRÉTATION SE VEUT PLEINE D'HUMOUR, TOUT COMME LA MODE DE TROTINETTE. (FRA)

▲ 25, 26 PHOTOS COLORÉES MAIN, TIRÉES SUR ILFORD GALERIE MATT, POUR UNE CAMPAGNE D'IMAGE D'ORELL FÜSSLI, QUI ÉDITE DIVERS MAGAZINES ET LIVRES. (SWI)

PHOTOGRAPHER:

DOMINICK GUILLEMOT

CAMERA:

PENTAX 6X7, NIKON

CLIENT:

GUESS?, INC.

ART DIRECTOR:

PAUL MARCIANO

DESIGNER:

SAMANTHA GIBSON

AGENCY:

GUESS?, INC.

IN-HOUSE

< 27

PHOTOGRAPHER:

KLAUS KAMPERT

CLIENT:

JÜRGEN NEBE MODE-

DESIGN

ART DIRECTOR:

KLAUS KAMPERT

28

■ 27 THE MAIN OBJECTIVE OF THIS PHOTO-GRAPH WAS TO HIGHLIGHT THE GUESS? FALL COLLECTION. BEING SCHEDULED IN WINTER, JAMAICA WAS CHOSEN FOR ITS SUNNY AND CLEAR CLIMATE. (USA)

■ 28 THIS PHOTOGRAPH FOR AN AD CAMPAIGN FOR A FASHION DESIGNER HIGHLIGHTS THE MAIN FEATURES OF THE COLLECTION: STYLE, CUT, FABRIC, AND QUALITY. (GER)

● 27 AUFNAHME DER HERBSTKOLLEKTION VON GUESS?. DA DIE AUFNAHMEN IM WINTER REA-LISIERT WERDEN SOLLTEN, WURDE JAMAICA WEGEN DES SONNIGEN, KLAREN KLIMAS ALS AUFNAHMEORT GEWÄHLT. (USA)

● 28 DIESE AUFNAHME AUS EINER WERBE-KAMPAGNE FÜR EINE MODEFIRMA VISUALI-SIERT DAS WESENTLICHE DER KOLLEKTION: STIL, SCHNITT, MATERIAL, QUALITÄT. (GER)

▲ 27 PHOTO DE LA COLLECTION AUTOMNE/HIVER DE GUESS?. AYANT DÛ ÊTRE RÉAL-ISÉES EN HIVER, LES PHOTOS FURENT PRISES À LA JAMAIQUE, À CAUSE DU CLIMAT CHAUD ET ENSOLEILLÉ DE CE PAYS. (USA)

▲ 28 CETTE PHOTO POUR UNE CAMPAGNE D'UNE MAISON DE MODE VISUALISE LES POINTS FORTS DE CETTE COLLECTION: STYLE, COUPE, MATIÈRE ET QUALITÉ. (GER)

PHOTOGRAPHER:

MARTIN RIEDL

REPRESENTATIVE:

DAVID LAMBERT

CAMERA:

SINAR 4X5

FILM:

ILFORD XP4

CLIENT:

LORO PIANA

ART DIRECTORS:

MICHAEL GÖTTSCHE,

VIVIDE PONZANI

AGENCY:

PIRELLA

GÖTTSCHE LOWE

< 29

PHOTOGRAPHER:

DIRK KARSTEN

REPRESENTATIVE:

ART PRODUCTION-

TEAM

30

PHOTOGRAPHER:

JOST WILDBOLZ

CAMERA:

PENTAX 6X7

FILM:

EKTACHROME 200

CLIENT:

SCHNEIDERS

BEKLEIDUNG

ART DIRECTOR:

FRANZ MERLICEK

DESIGNER:

JANNA THÜR

AGENCY:

DEMNER &

MERLICEK

31

■ 29 WITH THIS IMAGE, THE CASHMERE HOUSE IN MILAN, LORO PIANA WANTED TO CREATE THE FEELING OF QUALITY AMD TIMELESSNESS COMMONLY ASSOCIATED WITH BRITISH ARISTOCRACY AND PUBLIC SCHOOLS. (ITA)

■ 30 THE MODEL IN THIS PHOTOGRAPH IS A BODYBUILDER. IT SERVED AS SELF-PROMOTION FOR THE PHOTOGRAPHER. (GER)

■ 31 "JUMPING AT ONE'S OWN RISK"—THIS SIGN SERVED AS A HUMOROUS CONTRAST TO THE AESTHETICS OF THE FASHION PHOTOGRAPH WHICH APPEARED IN THE 91 SPRING/SUMMER BROCHURE FOR AN AUSTRIAN FASHION HOUSE. (AUT)

● 29 MIT DIESER AUFNAHME FÜR DAS KASCHMIR-HAUS LORO PIANA IN MAILAND SOLLTE DAS MIT BRITISCHEM ADEL UND SCHULEN ASSOZIIERTE GEFÜHL VON QUALITÄT VERMITTELT WERDEN. (ITA)

● 30 DAS MODELL FÜR DIESE AUFNAHME WAR EIN BODYBUILDER. DER PHOTOGRAPH VERWENDET SIE ALS EIGENWERBUNG. (GER)

● 31 DIE WARNUNG AM SPRUNGTURM DIENTE ALS HUMORVOLLER KONTRAST ZUR ÄSTHETIK DER MODEAUFNAHME, DIE IM KOLLEKTIONSPROSPEKT FRÜHJAHR/SOMMER 91 DER ÖSTERREICHISCHEN FIRMA SCHNEIDERS BEKLEIDUNG VERWENDET WURDE. (AUT)

▲ 29 CETTE PHOTO POUR LA MAISON LORO PIANA, SPÉCIALISÉE DANS LE CACHEMIRE, DEVAIT COMMUNIQUER UN SENTIMENT DE QUALITÉ, ASSOCIÉ À L'ARISTOCRATIE ANGLAISE ET À SES PENSIONNATS. (ITA)

▲ 30 LE MODÈLE DE CETTE PHOTO EST UN CULTURISTE. LE PHOTOGRAPHE L'A UTILISÉE POUR SON AUTOPROMOTION. (GER)

▲ 31 «TOUT PLONGEON EST À VOS PROPRES RISQUES»: L'AVERTISSEMENT FOURNISSAIT UN CONTRASTE PLEIN D'HUMOUR AVEC L'ESTHÉTIQUE DE CETTE PHOTO DE MODE QUI FIGURE DANS LE CATALOGUE PRINTEMPS/ÉTÉ 91 DE LA MAISON SCHNEIDER. (AUT)

PHOTOGRAPHER:

HANS HANSEN

CLIENT:

ENKA KG

ART DIRECTOR:

DETLEF BLUME

AGENCY:

STRUWE & PARTNER

32

PHOTOGRAPHER:

IVO VON RENNER

CAMERA:

NIKON F4

FILM:

KODAK EKTACHROME 64

PUBLISHER:

COUNTRY,

JAHRESZEITEN VERLAG

> 33

■ **32** THE SUBTLENESS OF VISCOSE FABRIC WAS PRESENTED IN A BOOK FOR ENKA KG, A PRODUCER OF FIBRES AND YARNS. (GER)

■ **33** THIS FASHION PHOTOGRAPH FOR *COUNTRY* MAGAZINE WAS TAKEN AT NIGHT AND COMPLETELY LIT BY FLASH. A FARM IN NORTH GERMANY WAS CHOSEN FOR LOCATION TO UNDERSCORE THE COUNTRYSIDE CHARACTER OF THE SERIES. (GER)

● **32** DIE GESCHMEIDIGKEIT VON VISKOSE-STOFFEN, DARGESTELLT IN EINEM BUCH FÜR DIE FASERHERSTELLERIN ENKA KG. (GER)

● **33** DIESE MODEAUFNAHME FÜR DIE ZEIT-SCHRIFT *COUNTRY* ENTSTAND NACHTS MIT BLITZLICHT. UM DEN LÄNDLICHEN CHARAKTER DER SERIE ZU UNTERSTREICHEN, WURDE GUT HASSELBURG IN NORDDEUTSCHLAND ALS AUF-NAHMEORT GEWÄHLT. (GER)

▲ **32** LA SOUPLESSE DE L'ÉTOFFE DE VIS-COSE PRÉSENTÉE DANS UN LIVRE POUR LE FABRICANT DE FIBRES ENKA KG. (GER)

▲ **33** CETTE PHOTO DE MODE POUR LE MAGA-ZINE *COUNTRY* A ÉTÉ PRISE DE NUIT; ELLE EST TOTALEMENT ÉCLAIRÉE AU FLASH. GUT HASSELBURG A ÉTÉ CHOISI COMME LIEU DES PRISES DE VUE, AFIN DE SOULIGNER LE CA-RACTÈRE CAMPAGNARD. (GER)

PHOTOGRAPHER:
SUSAN BOWLUS
< 34

PHOTOGRAPHER: CLIENT:
MARVY!/   THE LEE COMPANY
SHAWN MICHIENZI   ART DIRECTOR:
CAMERA: ARTY TAN
SINAR 8X10   DESIGNER:
FILM: ARTY TAN
KODAK   AGENCY:
EKTACHROME 64 T   FALLON MCELLIGOTT
                     35, 36

■ 34 PHOTOGRAPH SERVING AS SELF-PROMO-TION OF LOS ANGELES BASED PHOTOGRAPHER SUSAN BOWLUS. (USA)

■ 35, 36 THESE VIEWS OF LADIES' LIGHT-WEIGHT DENIM JEANS WERE PHOTOGRAPHED IN STUDIO-BUILT SETS. THE IMAGES WERE ASSIGNED FOR A LEE JEANS ADVERTISING CAMPAIGN. (USA)

● 34 AUS EINER REIHE VON AUFNAHMEN, DIE ALS EIGENWERBUNG DER PHOTOGRAPHIN SUSAN BOWLUS DIENTEN. (USA)

● 35, 36 DIESE ANSICHTEN LEICHTGEWICH-TIGER JEANS FÜR DAMEN WURDEN IN SPE-ZIELLEN AUFBAUTEN PHOTOGRAPHIERT. SIE GEHÖREN ZU EINER WERBEKAMPAGNE FÜR LEE-JEANS. (USA)

▲ 34 D'UNE SÉRIE DE PHOTOS UTILISÉES PAR LA PHOTOGRAPHE SUSAN BOWLUS POUR SON AUTOPROMOTION. (USA)

▲ 35, 36 CETTE PRÉSENTATION ORIGINALE DE JEANS LÉGERS POUR FEMMES A ÉTÉ RÉALI-SÉE DANS DES DÉCORS CONÇUS SPÉCIALE-MENT. CES PHOTOS FONT PARTIE D'UNE CAM-PAGNE POUR LES JEANS LEE. (USA)

PHOTOGRAPHER:
YANN ARTHUS
BERTRAND
CAMERA:
NAMIYA RZ67
PUBLISHER:
LUI
ART DIRECTOR:
JACQUES PLE
STYLIST:
JIM DE LA TOUR
37

PHOTOGRAPHER:
NORITSUNE NOSÉ
ART DIRECTOR:
NORITSUNE NOSÉ
DESIGNER:
NORITSUNE NOSÉ
STYLIST:
TOKIHIKO SHIN
MAKEUP HAIR:
YUMIKO UMEDA
> 38

■ 37 PHOTOGRAPH FROM AN ETHNOLOGICAL FASHION FEATURE IN *LUI* MAGAZINE. THE ASSIGNMENT WAS TO PRESENT EXOTIC LOOKING SWIMMING TRUNKS. IT WAS DECIDED TO HAVE HULIS, A TRIBE FROM PAPUA, NEW GUINEA, WEAR THEM. (FRA)

■ 38 SELF-ASSIGNED PORTRAIT OF A WOMAN WHO IS A PROFESSIONAL MODEL. (JPN)

● 37 AUS EINER «ETHNO-MODEREPORTAGE» FÜR *LUI*. ES GING UM DIE PRÄSENTATION EXOTISCH AUSSEHENDER BADEHOSEN. MAN BESCHLOSS, DIESE VON ANGEHÖRIGEN DES STAMMES DER HULIS AUS PAPUA IN NEUGUINEA TRAGEN ZU LASSEN. (FRA)

● 38 IM EIGENAUFTRAG ENTSTANDENES PORTRÄT EINER JUNGEN FRAU. (JPN)

▲ 37 PHOTO D'UN «ETHNO-REPORTAGE DE MODE» PUBLIÉ DANS *LUI*. IL S'AGISSAIT AU DÉPART DE PRÉSENTER DES MAILLOTS DE BAIN D'UN LOOK EXOTIQUE; IL FUT DÉCIDÉ DE FAIRE PORTER CES MODÈLES PAR UNE TRIBU DE PAPOUS, LES HULIS. (FRA)

▲ 38 PORTRAIT D'UNE JEUNE FEMME, RÉALISÉ COMME ÉTUDE PERSONNELLE. (JPN)

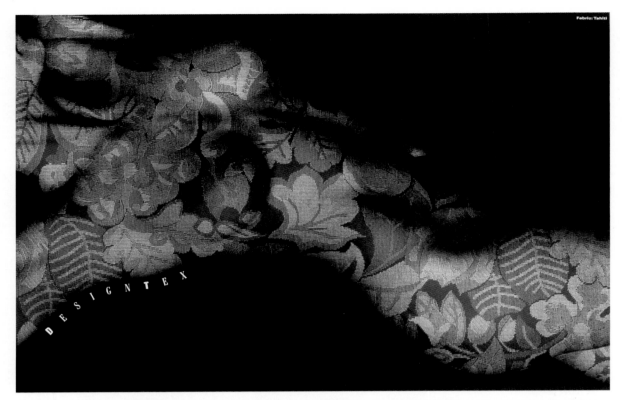

Fabric: Tahiti

DESIGNTEX

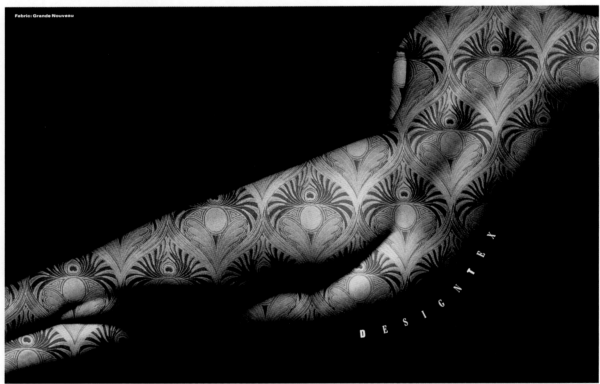

Fabric: Grande Nouveau

DESIGNTEX

PHOTOGRAPHER: ART DIRECTOR:
DON PENNY   RICK BIEDEL
CAMERA: DESIGNER:
PENTAX 6X7   RICK BIEDEL
FILM: AGENCY:
KODAK TRI-X   BONNELL DESIGN
CLIENT: ASSOCIATES
DESIGNTEX   39, 40

PHOTOGRAPHER: ART DIRECTORS:
JAVIER VALLHONRAT   ALBERTO NODOLINI,
REPRESENTATIVE: BENITA RAPHAN
MICHELE FILOMENO   DESIGNER:
PUBLISHER: BENITA RAPHAN
VOGUE ITALIA   STUDIO:
CLIENT: MICHELE FILOMENO
AGENCE FAM/   > 41
FABIENNE MARTIN

PHOTOGRAPHER:

PETER LINDBERGH

REPRESENTATIVE:

MARION DE BEAUPRE'

PROD.

CLIENT:

ALBERTO ASPESI

WOMAN

ART DIRECTOR:

FRANCA SONCINI

PIPPO RONDOLOTTI

DESIGNER:

PIPPO RONDOLOTTI

STYLIST:

ELISABETTE DIJAN

AGENCY:

SONCINI & GINEPRO

< 42

PHOTOGRAPHER:

BARBARA COLE

REPRESENTATIVE:

JANE CORKIN

GALLERY

CAMERA:

POLAROID

FILM:

SPECTRA

43

■ 42 ONE OF THE FULL-PAGE PHOTOGRAPHS FOR A FASHION CATALOG FOR THE SPRING/SUMMER 91 COLLECTION OF ALBERTO APESI ADDRESSED TO THE PRESS AND SHOPS. (ITA)

■ 43 "SAHARA"—THIS PHOTOGRAPH WAS TAKEN WITH AN INSTANT POLAROID CAMERA. THE PHOTOGRAPHER BARBARA COLE CHOSE SPECTRA FILM FOR ITS RICH COLOR PALETTE WHICH SHE ENHANCED BY USING WARM GELS OVER THE LIGHTS. (CAN)

● 42 EINE DER GANZSEITIG REPRODUZIERTEN AUFNAHMEN AUS EINEM FÜR PRESSE UND EINZELHANDEL BESTIMMTEN DAMENMODE-KATALOG FRÜHJAHR/SOMMER 91. (ITA).

● 43 «SAHARA» – DIE PHOTOGRAPHIN BARBARA COLE BENUTZTE EINE POLAROID-INSTANT-KAMERA MIT SPECTRA-FILM WEGEN DER SATTEN FARBWERTE, DIE SIE DURCH VERWENDUNG WARMER FILTER AUF DEN LAMPEN NOCH VERSTÄRKTE. (CAN)

▲ 42 L'UNE DES PHOTOS REPRODUITES SUR PLEINE PAGE DANS UN CATALOGUE DE MODE FÉMININE DESTINÉ À LA PRESSE ET AUX DÉTAILLANTS. (ITA)

▲ 43 «SAHARA». LA PHOTOGRAPHE A CHOISI D'UTILISER UN APPAREIL POLAROÏD. AVEC UN FILM SPECTRA À CAUSE DE SES COULEURS SATURÉES, QU'ELLE A ENCORE ACCENTUÉES EN ÉTENDANT DES FILTRES EN GÉLATINE DE TONS CHAUDS SUR LES LAMPES. (CAN)

JOURNALISM

JOURNALISMUS

JOURNALISME

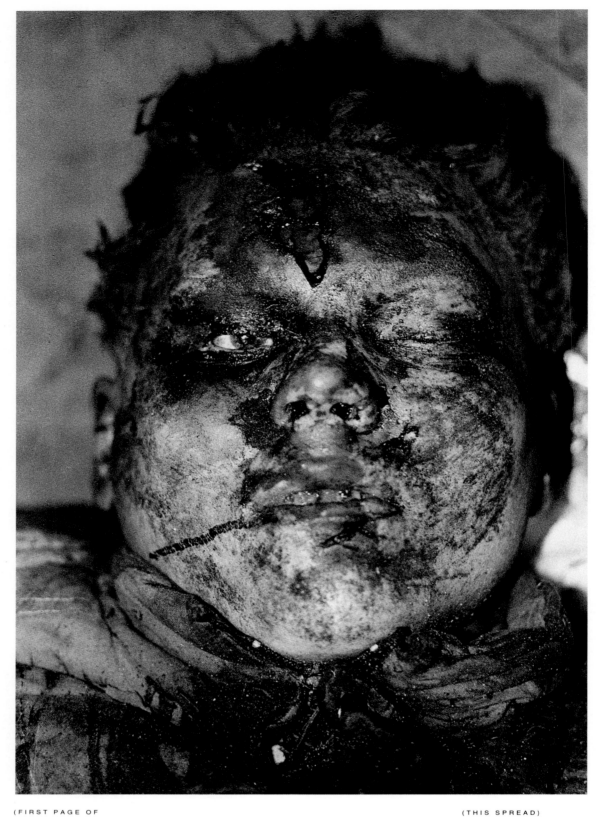

(FIRST PAGE OF
JOURNALISM SECTION)
PHOTOGRAPHER:
JOHN RUNNING
PUBLISHER:
NORTHLAND
PUBLISHING
DESIGNER:
DAVID JENNY
< 44

(THIS SPREAD)
PHOTOGRAPHER:
ROMUALDAS POZERSKIS
REPRESENTATIVE:
LITHUANIAN PHOTO-
GRAPHERS UNION
CAMERA:
MINOLTA X 700
FILM:
SVEMA, KODAK, ILFORD
45-47

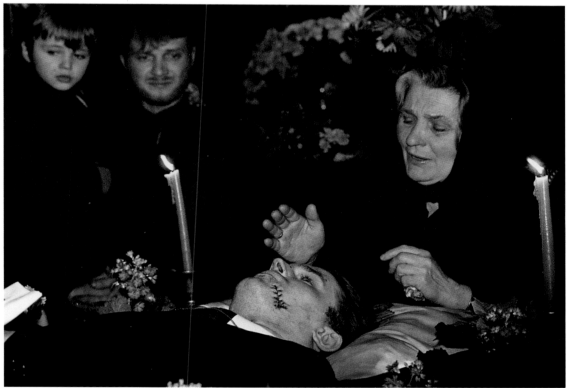

■ 44 (FIRST PAGE OF JOURNALISM SECTION) THE PAINTING IN THIS PHOTO, TAKEN IN JORDAN, IS A TRIBUTE TO NENA NABULSI, A SCHOOLGIRL SHOT BY THE ISRAELIS. (USA)

■ 45-47 (THIS SPREAD) "BLOODY SUNDAY IN LITHUANIA," A DOCUMENTATION OF THE VARIOUS EVENTS OF JANUARY 13, 1991. (LIT)

● 44 (ERSTE SEITE) DAS BILD IN DIESER AUFNAHME ZEIGT NENA NABULSI, EIN SCHULMÄDCHEN, DAS VON DEN ISRAELIS BEI BETHLEHEM ERSCHOSSEN WURDE. (USA)

● 45-47 (DIESE DOPPELSEITE) «BLUTIGER SONNTAG IN LITAUEN», EINE DOKUMENTATION DER EREIGNISSE AM 13. JANUAR 1991. (LIT)

▲ 44 (PREMIÈRE PAGE) LE TABLEAU QUE L'ON VOIT SUR CETTE PHOTO REPRÉSENTE NENA NABULSI, UNE ÉCOLIÈRE ABATTUE PAR LES ISRAÉLIENS PRES DE BETHLÉEM. (USA)

▲ 45-47 (CETTE DOUBLE PAGE) «DIMANCHE SANGLANT EN LITUANIE», UN DOCUMENT DES ÉVÉNEMENTS DU 13 JANVIER 1991. (LIT)

(PREVIOUS SPREAD)
PHOTOGRAPHER:
GEORGES MERILLON
REPRESENTATIVE:
AGENCE GAMMA
< 48

PHOTOGRAPHER:
STÉPHANE COMPOINT
REPRESENTATIVE:
SIGMA
ART DIRECTOR:
DAS MAGAZIN
DESIGNER:
OTHMAR ROTHENFLUH
49

PHOTOGRAPHER:
RONALD OLSHWANGER
CAMERA:
MINOLTA X-700
FILM:
AGFA 400
CLIENT:
MINOLTA CAMERA
CO., LTD.
ART DIRECTOR:
FRED O. BECHLEN
DESIGNER:
FRED O. BECHLEN
> 50

■ 48 (PREVIOUS SPREAD) A VICTIM OF THE CIVIL WAR IN YUGOSLAVIA, PHOTOGRAPHED IN KOSOVO. (FRA))

■ 49 FROM A REPORTAGE ON THE EXTINCTION OF THE BURNING OIL WELLS IN KUWAIT, A RESULT OF THE GULF WAR IN 1991. HERE ARE FIREMEN WHO ARE EXHAUSTED BY THE MUD, THE HEAT, THE NOISE, AND GASES. (SWI)

■ 50 RONALD OLSHWANGER IS AN AMATEUR PHOTOGRAPHER WHO HAS BEEN FOLLOWING FIRE TRUCKS WITH A CAMERA FOR 30 YEARS. HIS PICTURE OF FIREFIGHTER ADAM LONG RESCUING AN UNCONSCIOUS TWO-YEAR-OLD GIRL HAS WON HIM THE PULITZER PRIZE FOR SPOT-NEWS PHOTOGRAPHY. (JPN)

● 48 (VORANGEHENDE DOPPELSEITE) EIN OPFER DES BÜRGERKRIEGS IN JUGOSLAWIEN, AUFGENOMMEN IN KOSOVO. (FRA)

● 49 AUS EINER REPORTAGE ÜBER DAS LÖSCHEN DER BRENNENDEN ÖLFELDER IN KUWAIT. ÖLMATSCHE, HITZE, LÄRM, GESTANK UND GASE FÜHREN ZU ERSCHÖPFUNGSZUSTÄNDEN DER LÖSCHMANNSCHAFT. (SWI)

● 50 RONALD OLSHWANGER, EIN AMATEURPHOTOGRAPH, FOLGT SEIT DREISSIG JAHREN MIT SEINER KAMERA DER FEUERWEHR. SEINE AUFNAHME DIESES FEUERWEHRMANNS, DER EIN BEWUSSTLOSES ZWEIJÄHRIGES MÄDCHEN AUS DEN FLAMMEN RETTETE, WURDE MIT DEM PULITZER PREIS AUSGEZEICHNET. (JPN)

▲ 48 (DOUBLE PAGE PRÉCÉDENTE) UNE VICTIME DE LA GUERRE CIVILE EN YOUGOSLAVIE; LA PHOTO A ÉTÉ PRISE AU KOSOVO. (FRA)

▲ 49 D'UN REPORTAGE SUR L'EXTINCTION DES INCENDIES DE PUITS DE PÉTROLE AU KOWEIT, PROVOQUÉS PAR L'AGRESSEUR IRAKIEN LORS DE LA GUERRE DU GOLF. UN POMPIER S'ÉCROULE, ÉPUISÉ DE FATIGUE. (SWI)

▲ 50 RONALD OLSHWANGER EST UN PHOTOGRAPHE AMATEUR QUI, DEPUIS TRENTE ANS, DOCUMENTE LES INTERVENTIONS DE SAPEURS-POMPIERS. CETTE PHOTO D'UN POMPIER SAUVANT DES FLAMMES UNE FILLETTE DE DEUX ANS ÉVANOUIE A ÉTÉ RÉCOMPENSÉE PAR LE PRIX PULITZER. (JPN)

STILL LIFE

STILLEBEN

NATURE MORTE

BEST STILL LIFE

(FIRST PAGE OF

STILL LIFE SECTION)

PHOTOGRAPHER:

JONATHAN LOVEKIN

REPRESENTATIVE:

CAROL ACEY

BACKGROUND ARTIST:

SOPHIE KELLY

< 51

PHOTOGRAPHER:

LUCA PERAZZOLI

CAMERA:

TOYO 8X10

FILM:

KODAK

CLIENT:

FEDER LEASING

ART DIRECTOR:

ELEONORA GAROSCI

BACKDROPS:

LAURA ARDUIN

AGENCY:

IMPACT DOLCI BIASI

52

PHOTOGRAPHER:
LUCA PERAZZOLI
CAMERA:
TOYO FIELD
8X10
FILM:
KODAK
ART DIRECTOR:
LUCA PERAZZOLI
53

■ **51** (FIRST PAGE OF STILL LIFE SECTION) PERSONAL WORK OF LONDON BASED PHOTOGRAPHER JONATHAN LOVEKIN. (GBR)

■ **52** THE FIRST OF A SERIES OF PHOTOGRAPHS COMMISSIONED FOR A MAGAZINE CAMPAIGN BY FEDER LEASING, A FINANCIAL INSTITUTE IN MILAN, THE BACKDROP WAS CREATED BY LAURA ARDUIN. (ITA)

■ **53** STILL LIFE WITH FIVE LILIES PHOTOGRAPHED FOR SELF-PROMOTION (KODAK FILM). THE GRAIN EFFECT WAS NOT OBTAINED IN THE DEVELOPING PROCESS. (ITA)

● **51** (ERSTE SEITE) FREIE ARBEIT UND EIGENWERBUNG DES LONDONER PHOTOGRAPHEN JONATHAN LOVEKIN. (GBR)

● **52** ERSTE AUFNAHME EINER REIHE, DIE VON DEM FINANZINSTITUT FEDER LEASING FÜR EINE MAGAZINKAMPAGNE IN AUFTRAG GEGEBEN WURDE. DER HINTERGRUND WURDE VON LAURA ARDUIN GESCHAFFEN. (ITA)

● **53** STILLEBEN, DAS DER PHOTOGRAPH ALS EIGENWERBUNG VERWENDETE. DER GROBKÖRNIGE EFFEKT WURDE NICHT BEIM ENTWICKLUNGSPROZESS ERZIELT. (ITA)

▲ **51** (PREMIÈRE PAGE) ÉTUDE PERSONNELLE UTILISÉE PAR LE PHOTOGRAPHE COMME AUTOPROMOTION. (GBR)

▲ **52** PREMIÈRE D'UNE SÉRIE DE PHOTOS RÉALISÉE POUR UNE CAMPAGNE DE MAGAZINE DE LA FEDER LEASING, UN INSTITUT DE CRÉDIT DE MILAN. LA TOILE DE FOND A ÉTÉ RÉALISÉE PAR LAURA ARDUIN. (ITA)

▲ **53** ÉTUDE PERSONNELLE DU PHOTOGRAPHE, QUI LUI SERT ÉGALEMENT D'AUTOPROMOTION. L'EFFET GRANULEUX DE LA PHOTO NE RÉSULTE PAS DE LA DUPLICATION. (ITA)

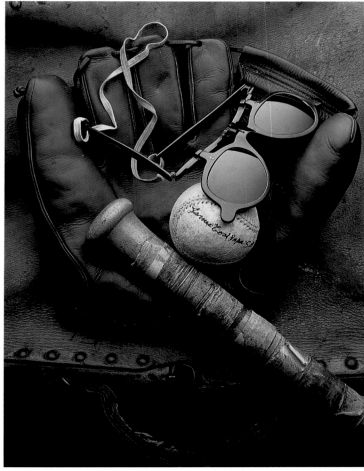

PHOTOGRAPHER:
DAN BONSEY
CAMERA:
SINAR 4X5
FILM:
AGFAPAN 100
ART DIRECTOR:
DAN BONSEY
< 54

PHOTOGRAPHER:
DAVE JORDANO
REPRESENTATIVE:
VINCE KAMIN & ASSOC.
CAMERA:
SINAR 8X10
FILM:
POLAROID 809
ART DIRECTOR:
BART CROSBY
DESIGNER:
JANET GULLEY
AGENCY:
CROSBY ASSOC. INC.
55

PHOTOGRAPHER:
TERRY HEFFERNAN
CLIENT:
CONSOLIDATED PAPER
COMPANY
ART DIRECTORS:
LESLEE AVCHEN,
LAURA JACOBI
DESIGNER:
LESLEE AVCHEN·
56

■ 54 COMPOSITION OF NATURAL AND MAN-MADE SHAPES. THE BLOSSOM OF THE LILY WAS MEANT TO GLOW WHILE THE LEAVES, STEM, AND VASE WERE RESTRICTED TO NEGATIVE FORMS. (USA)

■ 55 "WINTER"—ONE OF FOUR PHOTOGRAPHS FOR SEASONAL POSTERS TO PROMOTE POLAROID TRANSFER PRINTS. THEY WERE USED AS SELF-PROMOTION. (USA)

■ 56 BASEBALL MEMORABILIA OF JAMES "COOL PAPA" BELL, ONE OF THE FIRST BLACK LEAGUERS TO BE ACCEPTED IN THE BASEBALL HALL OF FAME IN COOPERSTOWN, N.Y. THE PHOTOGRAPH WAS USED IN A BROCHURE TO PROMOTE THE PRINTING QUALITY OF CONSO-LITH GLOSS, A PRODUCT OF CONSOLIDATED PAPER COMPANY. (USA)

● 54 KOMPOSITION VON NATÜRLICHEN UND VOM MENSCHEN GESCHAFFENEN FORMEN. DIE BLÜTE DER LILIE WURDE ERLEUCHTET WÄHREND STENGEL, BLÄTTER UND VASE NUR ALS NEGATIVE FORMEN ERSCHEINEN. (USA)

● 55 «WINTER» – EINE DER AUFNAHMEN FÜR PLAKATE ZUM THEMA JAHRESZEITEN. WERBUNG FÜR POLAROID TRANSFER PRINTS DES PHOTOGRAPHEN. (USA)

● 56 SOUVENIRS EINES BERÜHMTEN AMERIKANISCHEN BASEBALLSPIELERS, JAMES «COOL PAPA» BELL, DER ERSTE SCHWARZE SPIELER, DER IN DIE BASEBALL HALL OF FAME IN COOPERSTOWN, N.Y., AUFGENOMMEN WURDE. DIE AUFNAHME STAMMT AUS EINER BROSCHÜRE FÜR DAS PAPIER CONSOLITH GLOSS DER CONSOLIDATED PAPER COMPANY. (USA)

▲ 54 COMPOSITION DE FORMES NATURELLES ET DE FORMES CRÉÉES PAR L'HOMME. LES FLEURS DE LYS ONT ÉTÉ ÉCLAIRÉES, TANDIS QUE LA TIGE, LES FEUILLES ET LE VASE APPARAISSENT EN NÉGATIF. (USA)

▲ 55 «HIVER» – PHOTO D'UNE SÉRIE POUR DES AFFICHES. ELLES SERVENT À PROMOUVOIR LE PROCÉDÉ DE TRANSFERT À PARTIR DE CLICHÉS POLAROÏD. (USA)

▲ 56 SOUVENIRS D'UN CÉLÈBRE JOUEUR DE BASE-BALL AMÉRICAIN, JAMES «COOL PAPA» BELL, L'UN DES PREMIERS NOIRS À ÊTRE HONORÉ AU BASEBALL HALL OF FAME DE COOPERSTOWN. CETTE PHOTO A ÉTÉ RÉALISÉE, AFIN DE METTRE EN VALEUR LES QUALITÉS PARTICULIÈRES DU PAPIER CONSOLITH GLOSS. (USA)

PHOTOGRAPHER:

CHRIS WIMPEY

CAMERA:

TOYO 45G

FILM:

POLAROID 59/

POLAROID 669

ART DIRECTOR:

CHRIS WIMPEY

DESIGNER:

CHRIS WIMPEY

57-59

■ 57-59 THREE PHOTOGRAPHS FROM A PORT-FOLIO OF IMAGES RELATING TO TIME AND CHANGE, AND TO THE CHANGING NATURE OF BEAUTY IN OBJECTS REVEALING ASPECTS PREVIOUSLY CONCEALED. (USA)

● 57-59 DREI AUFNAHMEN AUS EINER SERIE, DIE SICH MIT ZEIT UND VERÄNDERUNG BE-FASST, MIT DER SICH WANDELNDEN SCHÖN-HEIT IN DEN DINGEN UND DEN IHNEN INNE-WOHNENDEN VERBORGENEN ASPEKTEN. (USA)

▲ 57-59 TROIS EXEMPLES D'UNE SÉRIE DE PHOTOS QUI ONT POUR THÈME LE TEMPS ET LES ALTÉRATIONS QUE SUBISSENT LES BEAU-TÉS DE LA NATURE, RÉVÉLANT UN AUTRE AS-PECT DES CHOSES. (USA)

PHOTOGRAPHER:

THOMAS HOLLAR

CAMERA:

SINAR 4X5

FILM:

KODAK EKTACHROME

PUBLISHER:

KASMIER REIMERS

HOLLAR INC.

ART DIRECTOR:

BRUCE MAYO

DESIGNER:

RANDY NICKEL

60

PHOTOGRAPHER:

DOUGLAS BENEZRA

PUBLISHER:

PORTAL PUBLICATIONS

> 61

■ 60 FROM A SERIES OF STILL LIFES USED AS SELF-PROMOTION BY PHOTOGRAPHER THOMAS HOLLAR. (USA)

■ 61 ALTHOUGH THIS PHOTOGRAPH WAS SHOT IN BLACK-AND-WHITE IT WAS PRODUCED BY FOUR COLOR PROCESS. IT BELONGS TO A SERIES ASSIGNED BY PORTAL PUBLICATIONS TO BE SOLD AS QUALITY PRINTS. (USA)

● 60 AUS EINER REIHE VON STILLEBEN, DIE DER PHOTOGRAPH THOMAS HOLLAR ALS EIGENWERBUNG VERWENDET. (USA)

● 61 OBGLEICH IN SCHWARZWEISS PHOTOGRAPHIERT, WURDE DIESES STILLEBEN IM VIERFARBENPROZESS GEDRUCKT. ES GEHÖRT ZU EINER REIHE, DIE FÜR DEN VERKAUF BESTIMMT IST. (USA)

▲ 60 D'UNE SÉRIE DE NATURES MORTES UTILISÉE COMME AUTOPROMOTION PAR LE PHOTOGRAPHE THOMAS HOLLAR. (USA)

▲ 61 BIEN QU'ELLE AIT ÉTÉ PHOTOGRAPHIÉE EN NOIR ET BLANC, CETTE NATURE MORTE FUT IMPRIMÉE EN QUADRICHROMIE. ELLE FAIT PARTIE D'UNE SÉRIE DE PHOTOS DESTINÉE À LA VENTE. (USA)

PHOTOGRAPHER:

PARISH KOHANIM

REPRESENTATIVE:

ROSANNE KOHANIM

ART DIRECTOR:

PARISH KOHANIM

STUDIO

DESIGNER:

PARISH KOHANIM

STUDIO

62

PHOTOGRAPHER:

STEFANO BIANCHI

REPRESENTATIVE:

DIXON-NELSON

CAMERA:

SINAR F2

FILM:

KODAK VPL 10X12

ART DIRECTOR:

STEFANO BIANCHI

> 63, 64

■ 62 THIS PHOTOGRAPH IS PART OF A SERIES OF PERSONAL STUDIES OF FLOWERS TO BE PUBLISHED IN A BOOK. (USA)

■ 63, 64 SEVERAL EXPOSURES WERE USED FOR THE PHOTOGRAPH OF AN UMBRELLA. IT WAS HIGHLIGHTED BY DIRECT LIGHT, WHILE A SOFT LIGHT WAS CAST ON THE FLOOR. COLOR REFLECTIONS WERE CAUGHT ON THE BOTTOM OF THE GOBLET. ALL OF THE EFFECTS WERE ACHIEVED DIRECT WITH THE LIGHTING. (ITA)

● 62 DIESE AUFNAHME GEHÖRT ZU EINER REIHE PERSÖNLICHER BLUMENSTUDIEN, DIE IN EINEM BUCH ERSCHEINEN WERDEN. (USA)

● 63, 64 DIE AUFNAHME DES SCHIRMS ENT- STAND MIT MEHRFACHBELICHTUNGEN. DER SCHIRM BEKAM DIREKTES, DER BODEN WEI- CHES LICHT. FARBREFLEXIONEN WURDEN AUF DEM GRUND DES POKALS EINGEFANGEN. ALLE EFFEKTE ENTSTANDEN DIREKT MIT HILFE DER BELEUCHTUNG. (ITA)

▲ 62 CETTE PHOTO FAIT PARTIE D'UNE SÉRIE D'ÉTUDES PERSONNELLES DE FLEURS, QUI SERONT PUBLIÉES DANS UN LIVRE. (USA)

▲ 63, 64 CETTE PHOTO A NÉCESSITÉ DES EXPOSITIONS MULTIPLES. LE PARAPLUIE ÉTAIT SOUS UN ÉCLAIRAGE DIRECT, LE SOL DANS UNE LUMIÈRE DOUCE. LES REFLETS COLORÉS FURENT CAPTÉS AU FOND DE LA COUPE. TOUS LES EFFETS ONT ÉTÉ PRODUITS UNIQUEMENT À L'AIDE DE L'ÉCLAIRAGE. (ITA)

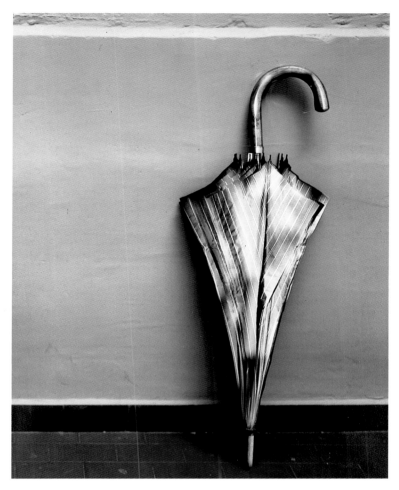

PHOTOGRAPHER:
DIETER KLEIN
CAMERA:
HASSELBLAD
FILM:
KODAK EKTACHROME
CLIENT:
MUSEUMSGESELLSCHAFT
BRÜHL E.V.
65, 66

PHOTOGRAPHER:
PARISH KOHANIM
REPRESENTATIVE:
ROSANNE KOHANIM
ART DIRECTOR:
PARISH KOHANIM
DESIGNER:
PARISH KOHANIM
67

■ 65, 66 WOODEN KITCHEN UTENSILS—OBJECTS THAT ARE PART OF THE COLLECTION OF A MUSEUM IN BRÜHL WHICH IS IN THE COURSE OF CONSTRUCTION. IT WILL CONTAIN OBJECTS OF EVERYDAY CULTURE FROM THE 8TH CENTURY UP TO THE PRESENT. (GER)

● 65, 66 HÖLZERNE KÜCHENGERÄTE – OBJEKTE AUS DER SAMMLUNG DER MUSEUMSGESELLSCHAFT BRÜHL. DAS MUSEUM, DAS SICH IM AUFBAU BEFINDET, WIRD ALLTAGSGEGENSTÄNDE AUS DER ZEIT VOM 8. JAHRHUNDERT BIS HEUTE ENTHALTEN. (GER)

▲ 65, 69 USTENSILES DE CUISINE EN BOIS. CES OBJETS FONT PARTIE DE LA COLLECTION DU MUSÉE DE LA CULTURE QUOTIDIENNE À BRÜHL (ALLEMAGNE), QUI PRÉSENTERA DES OBJETS DE LA VIE COURANTE DU MOYEN ÂGE À NOS JOURS. (GER)

■ 67 PHOTOGRAPH FROM A SERIES OF PERSONAL WORK BY PARISH KOHANIM, TAKEN WITH EKTACHROME PROFESSIONAL PLUS FILM, PUSHED SEVERAL STOPS. (USA)

● 67 AUFNAHME AUS EINER REIHE PERSÖNLICHER STUDIEN VON PARISH KOHANIM. DER FILM, EKTACHROME PROFESSIONAL PLUS ISO 100, WURDE GESTOSSEN. (USA)

▲ 67 PHOTOGRAPHIE TIRÉE D'UNE SÉRIE D'ÉTUDES PERSONNELLES. LA PELLICULE EKTACHROME PROFESSIONAL PLUS A ÉTÉ POUSSÉE AU TIRAGE. (USA)

PHOTOGRAPHER:
TERRY HEFFERNAN
CAMERA:
SINAR P 8X10
FILM:
KODAK EKTACHROME
CLIENT:
HOME STAKE
MINING CO.

ART DIRECTORS:
DAVID BROOM,
KIM URBAIN
AGENCY:
BROOM & BROOM
< 68

PHOTOGRAPHER:
PHILIP BEKKER
CAMERA:
SINAR P 8X10
FILM:
POLAROID 809

ART DIRECTOR:
PHILIP BEKKER
DESIGNER:
PHILIP BEKKER
69

■ 68 FROM AN ANNUAL REPORT OF A MINING COMPANY DEPICTING VARIOUS ASPECTS OF THEIR GLOBAL BUSINESS. EVERY MORNING, A TRUCK BROUGHT SEVERAL BARS OF GOLD TO THE PHOTOGRAPHER'S STUDIO. (USA)

■ 69 FROM A STILL LIFE SERIES USING BONES, FLOWERS, AND FRUIT TO PROMOTE 8X10 POLAROID TRANSFER TECHNIQUE: POLAROID TYPE 809, TRANSFERRED TO ARCHES WATERCOLOR PAPER. (USA)

● 68 AUS DEM JAHRESBERICHT EINER BERG-BAUFIRMA, IN DEM ASPEKTE DES GLOBALEN UNTERNEHMENS AUFGEZEIGT WERDEN SOLL-TEN. JEDEN MORGEN BRACHTE EIN LASTWA-GEN DIEE GOLDBARREN INS STUDIO. (USA)

● 69 AUS EINER REIHE VON STILLEBEN, DIE ALS WERBUNG FÜR EINE 8X10 POLAROID-TRANSFER-TECHNIK VERWENDET WURDE. MATERIAL: POLAROID TYPE 809, AUF ARCHES AQUARELLPAPIER ÜBERTRAGEN. (USA)

▲ 68 D'UNE SÉRIE POUR LE RAPPORT ANNUEL D'UNE COMPAGNIE MINIÈRE, QUI PRÉSENTE LES MULTIPLES ASPECTS DE CETTE GRANDE SOCIÉTÉ. CHAQUE MATIN, UN CAMION APPOR-TAIT AU STUDIO LES LINGOTS D'OR. (USA)

▲ 69 D'UNE SÉRIE DE NATURES MORTES DES-TINÉE À PROMOUVOIR UN NOUVEAU PROCÉDÉ DE TRANSFERT À PARTIR DE PHOTOS POLAROÏD. (POLAROÏD TYPE 809, TIRÉES SUR PAPIER AQUARELLE ARCHES. (USA)

PHOTOGRAPHER:
EUGENE WEISBERG
REPRESENTATIVE:
BARBARA LIVENSTEIN
CAMERA:
SINAR 8X10 P2
FILM:
KODAK EKTACHROME
70

PHOTOGRAPHER:
FERNANDO LUIZ
CARRIERI
CAMERA:
SINAR P
FILM:
EKTACHROME 6
> 71, 72

■ 70 THE PASTEL COLORS OF THESE FLOWERS WORK WELL WITH THE PALETTE FOR THE VASE, AND THE IMPRESSIONISTIC BACKGROUND LENDS THIS PHOTOGRAPH A PAINTERLY QUALITY. (USA)

● 70 DIE PASTELLTÖNE DER BLUMEN, AUF DIE DIE VASE UND DER IMPRESSIONISTISCHE HINTERGRUND ABGESTIMMT WURDEN, VERLEIHEN DIESER AUFNAHME EINE MALERISCHE QUALITÄT. (USA)

▲ 70 LES TEINTES PASTEL DES FLEURS, QUI ONT DÉTERMINÉ LA COULEUR DU VASE ET LA TOILE DE FOND IMPRESSIONNISTE, CONFÈRENT À CETTE PHOTO UN CARACTÈRE PICTURAL. (USA)

■ 71, 72 THE PHOTOGRAPHER'S PERSONAL STUDIES USED FOR SELF-PROMOTION. (BRA)

● 71, 72 PERSÖNLICHE STUDIEN DES PHOTOGRAPHEN. (BRA)

▲ 71, 72 ÉTUDES PERSONNELLES DU PHOTOGRAPHE. (BRA)

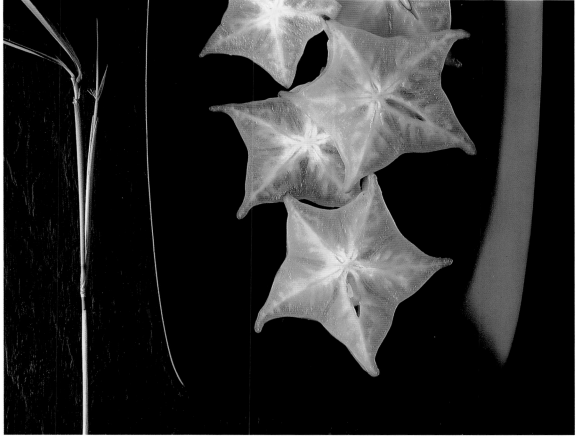

PHOTOGRAPHER:

ROGER CAMP

REPRESENTATIVE:

BLACK STAR

CAMERA:

OLYMPUS OM2

FILM:

KODACHROME 25

PUBLISHER:

AMBER LOTUS

ART DIRECTOR:

JERRY HOROVITZ

73

PHOTOGRAPHER:

NADAV KANDER

> 74

■ 73 THE FLOWERS, ALREADY DEAD OR JUST DYING, WERE PHOTOGRAPHED IN THE STUDIO UNDER A SKYLIGHT. (USA)

● 73 AUS EINER SERIE MIT DEM TITEL «STUDIO LIVES». DIE BLUMEN WURDEN IM STUDIO MIT TAGESLICHT PHOTOGRAPHIERT. (USA)

▲ 73 DE LA SÉRIE «STUDIO LIVES». LES FLEURS ONT ÉTÉ PHOTOGRAPHIÉES EN STUDIO SOUS UN ÉCLAIRAGE NATUREL. (USA)

■ 74 PERSONAL STUDY BY NADAV KANDER, USED AS SELF-PROMOTION. (GBR)

● 74 PERSÖNLICHE STUDIE DES PHOTOGRAPHEN NADAV KANDER. (GBR)

▲ 74 ETUDE PERSONNELLE DU PHOTOGRAPHE NADAV KANDER. (GBR)

FOOD

LEBENSMITTEL

CUISINE

(FIRST PAGE OF
FOOD SECTION)
PHOTOGRAPHER:
LES SZURKOWSKI
CAMERA:
HORSEMAN 450LX
FILM:
FUJI 100
CLIENTS:
GOODY COLOR
SEPARATION,
LS STUDIO,
DESIGN HOUSE INC.
C&C JOINT PRINTING
CO. LTD.
ART DIRECTOR:
LES SZURKOWSKI
DESIGNER:
LES SZURKOWSKI
AGENCY:
DESIGN HOUSE INC.
< 75

PHOTOGRAPHER:
ROGER PAPERNO
CAMERA:
LINHOF 4X5
FILM:
POLAROID 55
CLIENT:
CLOS DU BOIS WINERY
ART DIRECTOR:
LIZ HECKER
DESIGNER:
LIZ HECKER
< 76

PHOTOGRAPHER:
CAROL KAPLAN
REPRESENTATIVE:
ROBIN FERNSELL
CLIENT:
HEALTH AMERICA
ART DIRECTOR:
BETH WERTHER
AGENCY:
A. RICHARD JOHNSON
77, 78

■ 75 (FIRST PAGE OF FOOD SECTION) PHOTO-
GRAPH FROM A JOINT PROMOTIONAL CALEN-
DAR FOR FOUR COMPANIES. (CAN)

■ 76 THIS SIGNED PHOTOGRAPH, PRODUCED
IN A LIMITED EDITION, WAS TO ILLUSTRATE
THE CARE AND TENDERNESS THAT THE CLOS
DU BOIS WINERY HAS FOR ITS PRODUCT. IT
WAS LIT WITH A SINGLE SOFTBOX. (USA)

■ 77, 78 PHOTOGRAPHS FROM A HEALTHCARE
BROCHURE. THE NINE CONES SERVED AS A
METAPHOR FOR THE VARIETY OF HEALTH
PLANS AVAILABLE. THE SPIRAL CONE REPRE-
SENTS THE UPWARD SPIRALLING HEALTH
COSTS. (USA)

● 75 (ERSTE SEITE) AUS EINEM KALENDER
FÜR EINEN LITHOGRAPHEN, DRUCKER UND
PHOTOGRAPHEN. (CAN)

● 76 DIESE AUFNAHME (SIGNIERT, IN LIMI-
TIERTER AUFLAGE) SOLLTE DIE SORGFALT
UND LIEBE ZEIGEN, MIT DER DIE WINZEREI
MIT IHREM PRODUKT UMGEHT. BELEUCHTET
WURDE MIT EINER EINZIGEN SOFTBOX. (USA)

● 77, 78 AUFNAHMEN AUS EINER BROSCHÜRE
ÜBER DAS GESUNDHEITSWESEN. DIE NEUN
KUGELN DIENEN ALS METAPHER FÜR DIE VIEL-
ZAHL DER VORSORGEPROGRAMME. DIE SPIRA-
LE STEHT FÜR DIE WACHSENDEN KOSTEN DER
KRANKENPFLEGE. (USA)

▲ 75 (PREMIÈRE PAGE) D'UN CALENDRIER
PUBLIÉ PAR UN LITHOGRAPHE, UN IMPRIMEUR
ET UN PHOTOGRAPHE. (CAN)

▲ 76 IMAGE POLAROÏD (SIGNÉE, TIRAGE LIM-
ITÉ, RÉALISÉE À L'AIDE D'UNE SEULE SOFT-
BOX) POUR LE DOMAINE VITICOLE DU CLÔS
DU BOIS. ELLE ILLUSTRE L'AMOUR DU PRO-
DUCTEUR POUR SON PRODUIT. (USA)

▲ 77, 78 IMAGES TIRÉES D'UNE BROCHURE
SUR LA SANTÉ. LES NEUF CÔNES SONT UTIL-
ISÉES COMME MÉTAPHORES DE LA DIVERSITÉ
DU PROGRAMME DE PRÉVENTION. LA SPIRALE
SYMBOLISE LES COÛTS CROISSANTS DES
SOINS MÉDICAUX. (USA)

BEST FOOD

PHOTOGRAPHER:

ROSANNE OLSON

REPRESENTATIVE:

SANTEE LEHMEN

DABNEY INC.

CAMERA:

NIKON

FILM:

AGFACHROME 1000

ART DIRECTOR:

ROSANNE OLSON

79

■ 79 THIS STILL LIFE WAS PHOTOGRAPHED IN THE STUDIO USING AGFACHROME 1000 FILM AND TUNGSTEN LIGHTS. IT WAS USED FOR SELF-PROMOTION. (USA)

■ 80 BONES, FLOWERS, AND FRUIT WERE THE SUBJECTS OF A STILL LIFE SERIES WITH WHICH PHOTOGRAPHER PHILIP BEKKER WANTED TO PROMOTE HIS 8X10 POLAROID TRANSFER TECHNIQUE. (USA)

● 79 DIESES STILLEBEN WURDE IM STUDIO MIT AGFACHROME 1000 FILMMATERIAL UND TUNGSTENLICHT AUFGENOMMEN. ES DIENTE ALS EIGENWERBUNG. (USA)

● 80 KNOCHEN, BLUMEN UND FRÜCHTE SIND GEGENSTAND EINER REIHE VON STILLEBEN, MIT DENEN DER PHOTOGRAPH SEINE POLAROID-TRANSFER-TECHNIK DEMONSTRIEREN WOLLTE. (USA)

▲ 79 CETTE NATURE MORTE A ÉTÉ PRISE EN STUDIO AVEC UN ÉCLAIRAGE AU TUNGSTÈNE ET UNE PELLICULE AGFACHROME 1000. ELLE SERT D'AUTOPROMOTION. (USA)

▲ 80 DES OS, DES FLEURS ET DES FRUITS CONSTITUENT LE SUJET D'UNE SÉRIE DE NATURES MORTES, AU MOYEN DUQUEL LE PHOTOGRAPHE VOULAIT DÉMONTRER SA TECHNIQUE DE POLAROÏD TRANSFER. (USA)

PHOTOGRAPHER:
PHILIP BEKKER
FILM:
POLAROID 8X10
ART DIRECTOR:
PHILIP BEKKER
DESIGNER:
PHILIP BEKKER
STUDIO:
BEKKER
PHOTOGRAPHY
80

PHOTOGRAPHER:
LES SZURKOWSKI
CAMERA:
HORSEMAN 450LX
FILM:
FUJI 100
CLIENTS:
GOODY COLOR
SEPARATION,
LS STUDIO,
DESIGN HOUSE INC.
C&C JOINT PRINTING
CO. LTD.
ART DIRECTOR:
LES SZURKOWSKI
DESIGNER:
LES SZURKOWSKI
AGENCY:
DESIGN HOUSE INC.

81-85

■ 81-85 WITH THESE PHOTOGRAPHS USED IN A CALENDAR, A LITHOGRAPHER, A PRINTER, AND A PHOTOGRAPHER WANTED TO DEMON-STRATE THEIR CRAFTSMANSHIP. (CAN)

● 81-85 MIT DIESEN AUFNAHMEN FÜR EINEN KALENDER WOLLTEN EIN LITHOGRAPH, EIN DRUCKER UND EIN PHOTOGRAPH IHR KÖNNEN UNTER BEWEIS STELLEN. (CAN)

▲ 81-85 PHOTOS, REPRODUITES DANS UN CALENDRIER, ILLUSTRANT LE SAVOIR-FAIRE D'UN LITHOGRAPHE, D'UN IMPRIMEUR ET D'UN PHOTOGRAPHE. (CAN)

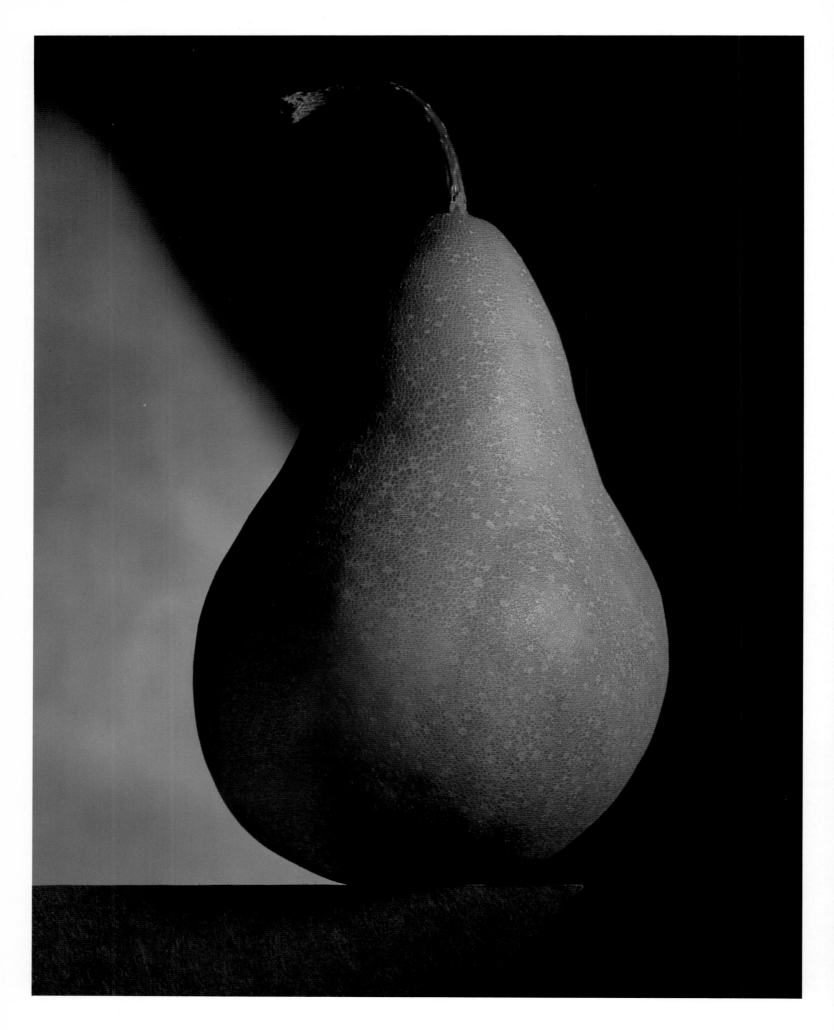

PHOTOGRAPHER:
JOEL CONISON
DESIGNER:
ROBIT PROBST
< 86

PHOTOGRAPHER:
KATHRYN KLEINMAN
CAMERA:
SINAR 8X10
FILM:
EKTACHROME 100 PLUS
CLIENT:
WATERFORD CRYSTAL
INC.
ART DIRECTOR:
RUSSLYN MILLS
STYLIST:
SARA SLAVIN
AGENCY:
AMMIRATI & PURIS
87

■ 86 SELF-PROMOTION FOR PHOTOGRAPHER JOEL CONISON OF CINCINNATI. (USA)

■ 87 THE AIM OF THIS PHOTOGRAPH, USED IN AN AD CAMPAIGN INTRODUCING A NEW LINE OF WATERFORD CRYSTAL, WAS TO SHOW THE BEAUTY OF CRYSTAL IN THE CONTEXT OF A SET TABLE. (USA)

● 86 EIGENWERBUNG DES PHOTOGRAPHEN JOEL CONISON AUS CINCINNATI. (USA)

● 87 MIT DIESER AUFNAHME SOLLTE DIE SCHÖNHEIT VON KRISTALL AUF DEM ESSTISCH DEMONSTRIERT WERDEN. SIE WURDE IN EINER KAMPAGNE FÜR EINE NEUE KRISTALL-LINIE VON WATERFORD VERWENDET. (USA)

▲ 86 AUTOPROMOTION D'UN PHOTOGRAPHE DE CINCINNATI, JOEL CONISON. (USA)

▲ 87 LA BEAUTÉ DU CRISTAL SUR UNE TABLE DE SALLE À MANGER. CETTE PHOTO A ÉTÉ UTILISÉE DANS UNE ANNONCE POUR LA PRO-MOTION D'UNE NOUVELLE LIGNE DE PRODUITS EN CRISTAL DE WATERFORD. (USA)

(TOP)

PHOTOGRAPHER:

NOB FUKUDA

PUBLISHER:

RIKUYO SHA CO. LTD.

ART DIRECTOR:

PETER ASSMANN

OUTLINE:

KOJI IKEDA

DESIGNER:

SUSUMU ENDO

AGENCY:

RIKUYO SHA CO. LTD.

88

(BOTTOM)

PHOTOGRAPHER:

NOB FUKUDA

CLIENT:

OSAKA YOMIURI

ADVERTISING CO. LTD.

CREATIVE DIRECTOR:

HIROKI NAKAGAMI

ART DIRECTOR:

HAJIME SHIMIZU

STYLIST:

TAKESI KADOKAMI

89

PHOTOGRAPHER:

GABY BRINK

STYLIST:

JO ANNE JOHNSON

90

■ 88 FOR THIS STILL LIFE PHOTOGRAPH LEAVES WERE STUCK TO POTS (FLOWER ARTIST: FRANZ JOSEF WEIN) CONTAINING PLANTS AND VEGETABLES. (JPN)

● 88 FÜR DIESES STILLEBEN WURDEN BLÄT-TER AUF DIE TÖPFE GEKLEBT (FLORIST: FRANZ JOSEF WEIN), DIE PFLANZEN UND GEMÜSE ENTHALTEN. (JPN)

▲ 88 POUR CETTE NATURE MORTE (FLEU-RISTE: FRANZ JOSEF WEIN), DES FEUILLES ONT ÉTÉ COLLÉES SUR DES POTS CONTENANT PLANTES ET LÉGUMES. (JPN)

■ 89 STILL LIFE FROM THE PHOTOGRAPHER'S PORTFOLIO. (JPN)

● 89 PERSÖNLICHE STUDIE DES PHOTOGRA-PHEN NOB FUKUDA. (JPN)

▲ 89 NATURE MORTE, DU PORTFOLIO DU PHO-TOGRAPHE NOB FUKUDA. (JPN)

■ 90 THIS STILL LIFE WAS USED AS SELF-PROMOTION BY PHOTOGRAPHER GABY BRINK OF OAKLAND. (USA)

● 90 DIESES STILLEBEN WURDE ALS EIGEN-WERBUNG DER PHOTOGRAPHIN GABY BRINK AUS OAKLAND VERWENDET. (USA)

▲ 90 CETTE NATURE MORTE A ÉTÉ UTILISÉE COMME AUTOPROMOTION PAR LA PHOTO-GRAPHE GABY BRINK, D'OAKLAND. (USA)

PEOPLE

MENSCHEN

PERSONNES

(FIRST PAGE OF
PEOPLE SECTION)
PHOTOGRAPHER:
FRANK W.
OCKENFELS 3
REPRESENTATIVE:
OUTLINE PRESS
PUBLISHER:
CREEM
< 91

PHOTOGRAPHER:
CAROL KAPLAN
REPRESENTATIVE:
ROBIN FERNSELL
STUDIO:
KAPLAN STUDIO, INC.
92

PHOTOGRAPHER:
MICHEL SABAH
CAMERA:
NIKON
CLIENT:
KONICA FRANCE
ART DIRECTOR:
OLIVIER D'ARFEUILLE
AGENCY:
SAINT-PAUL &
ASSOCIÉS
> 93

■ 91 (FIRST PAGE OF PEOPLE SECTION) A PORTRAIT OF ELVIS COSTELLO FOR *CREEM* MAGAZINE. MOST OF THE SHOOTING TOOK PLACE IN A PARK NEAR ELVIS' HOME IN LONDON, BUT THIS PICTURE WAS TAKEN IN THE PHOTOGRAPHER'S HOTEL ROOM. (USA)

■ 92 TWIN GIRLS LOOKING LIKE DOLLS. IMAGE USED AS SELF-PROMOTION FOR PHOTOGRAPHER CAROL KAPLAN. (USA)

■ 93 SENSIBLE, EFFICIENT, AND ENCHANTING—THIS WAS THE HEADLINE FOR AN ADVERTISEMENT FOR KONICA CAMERA, FOR WHICH THIS PHOTOGRAPH WAS ASSIGNED. (FRA)

● 91 (ERSTE SEITE) PORTRÄT VON ELVIS COSTELLO FÜR EIN INTERVIEW IN *CREEM*. WEGEN SCHLECHTER WETTERBEDINGUNGEN WURDE DIE AUFNAHME IM HOTELZIMMER DES PHOTOGRAPHEN STATT WIE VORGESEHEN IN EINEM LONDONER PARK GEMACHT. (USA)

● 92 ZWEI KLEINE MÄDCHEN, ZWILLINGE, DIE WIE PUPPEN AUSSEHEN. EIGENWERBUNG DER PHOTOGRAPHIN CAROL KAPLAN. (USA)

● 93 «SENSIBEL, EFFIZIENT UND ZAUBERHAFT» – SO DIE HEADLINE EINER ANZEIGE FÜR KONICA-KAMERAS, FÜR DIE DIESE AUFNAHME GEMACHT WURDE. (FRA)

▲ 91 (PREMIÈRE PAGE) PORTRAIT DU MUSICIEN ROCK ELVIS COSTELLO POUR UN REPORTAGE PUBLIÉ DANS LE MAGAZINE *CREEM*. EN RAISON DU MAUVAIS TEMPS, CELLE-CI FUT RÉALISÉE DANS LA CHAMBRE D'HÔTEL DU PHOTOGRAPHE. (USA)

▲ 92 JUMELLES QUI RESSEMBLENT À DES POUPÉES. AUTOPROMOTION DE LA PHOTOGRAPHE CAROL KAPLAN. (USA)

▲ 93 «SENSIBLE, EFFICACE ET MAGIQUE» – TEL EST LE GROS TITRE DE L'ANNONCE DE L'APPAREIL-PHOTO KONICA, POUR LAQUELLE CETTE IMAGE A ÉTÉ RÉALISÉE. (FRA)

PHOTOGRAPHER:
HELMUT NEWTON
PUBLISHER:
CONDÉ NAST TRAVELER
ART DIRECTOR:
DIANA LA GUARDIA
PHOTOGRAPHY DIRECTOR:
KATHLEEN KLECH
< 94

PHOTOGRAPHER:
MICHAEL O'BRIEN
REPRESENTATIVE:
MICHAEL ASH
CAMERA:
HASSELBLAD
FILM:
FUJI RDP
PUBLISHER:
NATIONAL GEOGRAPHIC
PHOTOGRAPHY DIRECTOR:
THOMAS R. KENNEDY
PICTURE EDITOR:
MARY G. SMITH
95

■ 94 A CAPRI TAXI DRIVER IN JUNE 1991. PHOTOGRAPHED FOR AN ARTICLE IN *CONDÉ NAST TRAVELER*. HE HAS DRIVEN ALL THE STARS THAT CAME TO NICE, PHOTOGRAPHER HELMUT NEWTON INCLUDED. (USA)

■ 95 ANNABELLE LARES, MISS AUSTIN 1989, PHOTOGRAPHED IN THREADGILL'S, A RESTAURANT WHERE JANIS JOPLIN'S CAREER STARTED. *NATIONAL GEOGRAPHIC* MAGAZINE ASSIGNED THE PHOTOGRAPHER TO DEPICT AUSTIN, TEXAS, THROUGH A CROSS SECTION OF ITS CITIZENS. (USA)

● 94 EIN TAXIFAHRER AUF CAPRI — AUS EINEM ARTIKEL IN DER ZEITSCHRIFT *CONDÉ NAST TRAVELER*. ER HAT ALLE STARS, DIE IN NIZZA WAREN, GEFAHREN, EINSCHLIESSLICH DES PHOTOGRAPHEN HELMUT NEWTON. (USA)

● 95 MISS AUSTIN, PHOTOGRAPHIERT IN THREADGILL'S, DEM RESTAURANT, IN DEM JANIS JOPLINS KARRIERE BEGANN. DER AUFTRAG DES MAGAZINS *NATIONAL GEOGRAPHIC* LAUTETE, AUSTIN, TEXAS, DURCH EINEN QUERSCHNITT SEINER BEVÖLKERUNG DARZUSTELLEN. (USA)

▲ 94 PHOTO PRISE À CAPRI, POUR UN ARTICLE PARU DANS *CONDÉ NAST TRAVELER*. CE CHAUFFEUR A CONDUIT TOUTES LES STARS QUI SONT VENUES À NICE, Y COMPRIS LE PHOTOGRAPHE HELMUT NEWTON. (USA)

▲ 95 LE *NATIONAL GEOGRAPHIC* MAGAZINE AVAIT DEMANDÉ AU PHOTOGRAPHE DE FAIRE UN REPORTAGE SUR LES HABITANTS D'AUSTIN, TEXAS. ANNABELLE LARES, MISS AUSTIN, EST ICI PHOTOGRAPHIÉE DANS LE RESTAURANT THREADGILL'S, OÙ JANIS JOPLIN FIT SES DÉBUTS. (USA)

PHOTOGRAPHER:

LINKEVICIUS KAZIMIERAS

CAMERA:

PENTACON SIX TL

FILM:

KODAK PANATOMIC X-32

96-98

■ 96-98 RICHLY DECORATED SOVIET MILITARY VETERANS: GORDIYEVSKY MITROFANOVICH, KRAPIVKO BORISOVICH AND ARKHIPOV ALEKSANROVICH. (LIT)

● 96-98 REICH DEKORIERTE VETERANEN DES SOWJETISCHEN MILITÄRS: GORDIYEVSKY MITROFANOVICH, KRAPIVKO BORISOVICH UND ARKHIPOV ALEKSANROVICH. (LIT)

▲ 96-98 VÉTÉRANS DE L'ARMÉE SOVIÉTIQUE, COUVERTS DE DÉCORATIONS: GORDIYEVSKY MITROFANOVICH, KRAPIVKO BORISOVICH ET ARKHIPOV ALEKSANROVICH. (LIT)

PHOTOGRAPHER:
TIM BIEBER
ART DIRECTOR:
TIM BIEBER
99

BEST PEOPLE
PHOTOGRAPHER:
HERB RITTS
REPRESENTATIVE:
VISAGES
ART DIRECTOR:
HERB RITTS
> 100

■ 99 OUT-TAKE FROM A CIGARETTE SHOOTING IN SOUTHERN MOROCCO. THE MAN WAS SITTING IN A DARK CAFE, ILLUMINATED ONLY BY THE LIGHT OF AN OIL LAMP. (USA)

● 99 DAS BILD ENTSTAND IN MAROKKO BEI AUFNAHMEN FÜR ZIGARETTENWERBUNG. DER MANN SASS IN EINEM DUNKLEN CAFÉ, NUR VOM LICHT DER ÖLLAMPE BELEUCHTET. (USA)

▲ 99 CETTE PHOTO A ÉTÉ RÉALISÉE DURANT DES PRISES DE VUE POUR UNE PUBLICITÉ DE CIGARETTES. L'ÉCLAIRAGE SE LIMITAIT À UNE SIMPLE LAMPE À HUILE. (USA)

■ 100 PHOTOGRAPH FROM A SERIES OF PORTRAITS OF DJIMON BY HERB RITTS. (USA)

● 100 DJIMONS PORTRÄT AUS EINER SERIE VON HERB RITTS. (USA)

▲ 100 PORTRAIT DE DJIMON, D'UNE SÉRIE DU PHOTOGRAPHE HERB RITTS. (USA)

PHOTOGRAPHER:
CHRISTINA HOPE
CAMERA:
NIKONOS
101-103

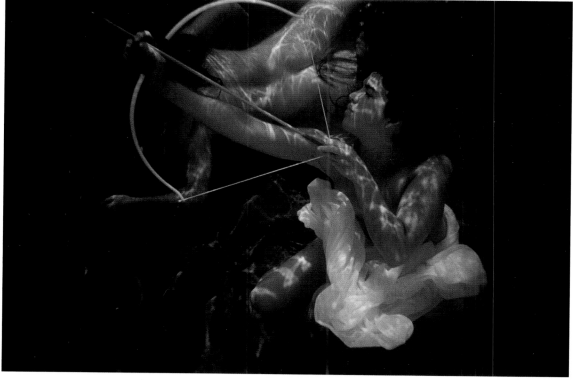

■ 101-103 THESE IMAGES ARE PART OF A SERIES FOR THE PHOTOGRAPER'S EXHIBITION AT THE JACKSONVILLE ART MUSEUM. THEY WERE USED FOR A POSTER AND INVITATIONS. THE PURPOSE OF THESE PHOTOGRAPHS IS TO TRANSPORT THE VIEWER INTO ANOTHER WORLD, IN WHICH ONE'S SENSES ARE CONCENTRATED ON THE PLAY OF NATURAL LIGHT AND SHADOW. THEY WERE TAKEN UNDER WATER IN A POOL. (USA)

● 101-103 DIESE IN EINEM SWIMMING POOL UNTER WASSER GEMACHTEN AUFNAHMEN GEHÖREN ZU EINER SERIE FÜR EINE AUSSTELLUNG DER PHOTOGRAPHIN. SIE WURDEN FÜR DAS PLAKAT UND EINLADUNGEN VERWENDET. MIT IHREN BILDERN MÖCHTE DIE PHOTOGRAPHIN DEN BETRACHTER IN EINE ANDERE WELT FÜHREN, EINE WELT IN DER SICH DIE SINNE AUF DAS NATÜRLICHE SPIEL VON LICHT UND SCHATTEN KONZENTRIEREN. (USA)

▲ 101-103 EXEMPLES D'UNE SÉRIE DE PHOTOS UTILISÉES ÉGALEMENT COMME AFFICHES ET CARTES D'INVITATION POUR UNE EXPOSITION PERSONNELLE AU MUSÉE DES BEAUX-ARTS DE JACKSONVILLE, EN FLORIDE. LA PHOTOGRAPHE CHERCHE À TRANSPORTER LE SPECTATEUR DANS UN AUTRE UNIVERS, SE ONCENTRANT SUR LES JEUX DE LUMIÈRE ET D'OMBRE: LES PHOTOS ONT ÉTÉ PRISES SOUS L'EAU, DANS UNE PISCINE. (USA)

PHOTOGRAPHER:
ROSANNE OLSON
REPRESENTATIVE:
SANTEE LEHMEN
DABNEY INC.
CAMERA:
HASSELBLAD
FILM:
T-MAX 100
ART DIRECTOR:
ROSANNE OLSON
104

PHOTOGRAPHER:
MICHAEL O'BRIEN
REPRESENTATIVE:
MICHAEL ASH
CAMERA:
HASSELBLAD
FILM:
KODAK EPP
PUBLISHER:
THE NEW YORK
TIMES MAGAZINE
ART DIRECTOR:
JANET FROELICH
PICTURE EDITOR:
KATHY RYAN
DESIGNER:
KANDY LITTRELL
> 105

■ 104 SEPIA-TONED-PORTRAIT OF URSULA B, PHOTOGRAPHED IN THE STUDIO WITH TUNGSTEN LIGHTS. (USA)

■ 105 "HEADSTRONG" WAS THE HEADLINE ON THE COVER OF *THE NEW YORK TIMES MAGAZINE* WHICH ASSIGNED THIS PORTRAIT OF BASKETBALL STAR CHARLES BARKLEY OF THE PHILADELPHIA 76ERS. (USA)

● 104 PORTRÄT IM SEPIATON VON URSULA B., AUFGENOMMEN IM STUDIO MIT TUNGSTEN-LICHT. (USA)

● 105 «KOPFSTARK» WAR DIE SCHLAGZEILE AUF DEM UMSCHLAG DES *NEW YORK TIMES MAGAZINE* MIT DIESEM PORTRAIT DES BASKETBALL-STAR CHARLES BARKLEY VON DEN PHILADELPHIA 76ERS. (USA)

▲ 104 PORTRAIT TIRÉ EN SÉPIA DE URSULA B., RÉALISÉ EN STUDIO À L'AIDE D'UN ÉCLAIRAGE AU TUNGSTÈNE. (USA)

▲ 105 LE CÉLÈBRE JOUEUR DE BASKET-BALL DE L'ÉQUIPE AMÉRICAINE DES PHILADELPHIA 76ERS, CHARLES BARKLEY; PHOTO PUBLIÉE EN COUVERTURE DU *NEW YORK TIMES MAGAZINE* SOUS LE TITRE «TÊTE DURE». (USA)

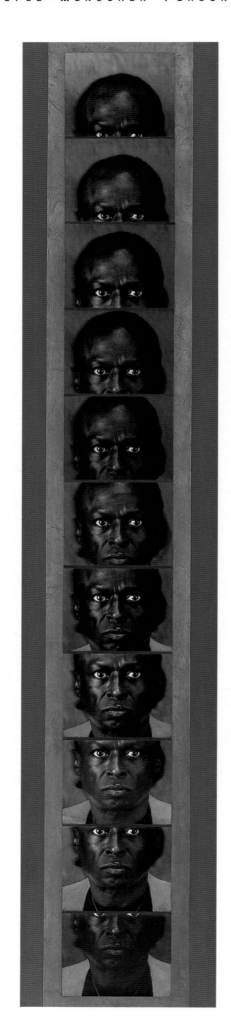

PHOTOGRAPHER:

GILLES LARRAIN

CAMERA:

ROLLEIFLEX SL 66E

PHOTO MONTAGE,

COLLAGE, AND PAINTING:

COCO LARRAIN,

GILLES LARRAIN

CLIENT:

THE MEADOWS MUSEUM

ART DIRECTORS:

ARTHUR EISENBERG,

SAUL TORRES

DESIGNER:

SAUL TORRES

AGENCY:

EISENBERG AND

ASSOCIATES

106, 107

■ 106, 107 "SUNSET AND DAWN" AND "THE USES OF ENCHANTMENT"—PHOTOGRAPHS FROM A CATALOG FOR AN EXHIBITION OF PHOTOGRAPHER GILLES LARRAIN AT THE MEADOWS MUSEUM OF DALLAS. (USA)

● 106, 107 «VON SONNENAUFGANG BIS SONNENUNTERGANG» UND «ANWENDUNGEN DER VERZAUBERUNG» – AUS EINEM KATALOG DES PHOTOGRAPHEN GILLES LARRAIN IM MEADOWS MUSEUM VON DALLAS. (USA)

▲ 106, 107 «DE L'AUBE AU CRÉPUSCULE» ET «LES USAGES DE LA MAGIE». PHOTOS D'UN CATALOGUE D'UNE EXPOSITION PERSONNELLE DU PHOTOGRAPHE GILLES LARRAIN AU MEADOWS MUSEUM DE DALLAS. (USA)

Photographer:

SUE BENNETT

Camera:

NIKON

Film:

TRI-X, NEOPAN

Publisher:

CBS/SONY

Art Director:

SUSUMU SHINOZAKI

Designer:

SUSUMU SHINOZAKI

Agency:

TOKYU AGENCY

INTERNATIONAL

108-111

■ 108-111 THESE PHOTOGRAPHS ARE PART OF A SERIES USED FOR COMPACT DISC COVERS OF COUNTRY WESTERN ARTISTS. THE COWBOYS, FROM VARIOUS RANCHES IN THE WESTERN UNITED STATES, WERE PHOTOGRAPHED WITH NATURAL LIGHT. (USA)

● 108-111 DIESE AUFNAHMEN GEHÖREN ZU EINER REIHE FÜR CD COVERS MIT COUNTRY-MUSIK. DIE COWBOYS STAMMEN VON VERSCHIEDENEN RANCHES IM WESTEN DER VEREINIGTEN STAATEN. SIE WURDEN BEI TAGESLICHT PHOTOGRAPHIERT. (USA)

▲ 108-111 D'UNE SÉRIE DE PHOTOS POUR LES COUVERTURES DE DISQUES-COMPACT DE COUNTRY MUSIC. DES COW-BOYS QUI TRAVAILLENT DANS DES RANCHES DE L'OUEST DES ÉTATS-UNIS ONT ÉTÉ PHOTOGRAPHIÉS DANS UN ÉCLAIRAGE NATUREL. (USA)

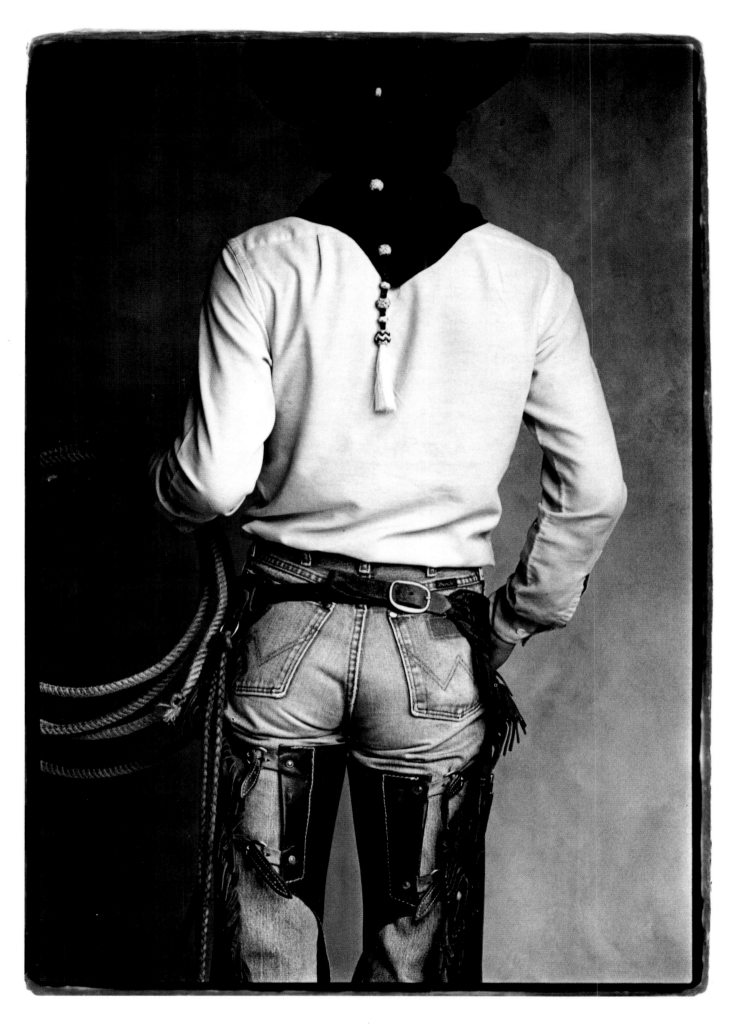

PHOTOGRAPHER:
ANDREW ECCLES
PUBLISHER:
LEAR'S
ART DIRECTOR:
JEANNE ARNOLD
DESIGN DIRECTOR:
RON ALBRECHT
< 112

PHOTOGRAPHER:
NEAL SLAVIN
PUBLISHER:
PC MAGAZINE
ART DIRECTOR:
ANNE BAYLOR
DESIGNER:
ANNE BAYLOR
AGENCY:
PAGANO
SCHENCK & KAY
113

■ 112 PORTRAIT OF DESIGNER/ILLUSTRA-TOR/ARTIST MILTON GLASER FOR *LEAR'S* MAGAZINE. (USA)

■ 113 "PC MAGAZINE ISN'T TAKEN AS GOSPEL BY ALL." PHOTOGRAPH FROM AN AD CAMPAIGN FOR *PC MAGAZINE* EMPHASIZING THAT IT IS MEANT FOR A SPECIAL READERSHIP. (USA)

● 112 PORTRÄT DES DESIGNERS/ ILLUSTRA-TORS/KÜNSTLERS MILTON GLASER FÜR DIE ZEITSCHRIFT *LEAR'S*. (USA)

● 113 DIESE AUFNAHME STAMMT AUS EINER WERBEKAMPAGNE FÜR *PC MAGAZINE*, DAS SICH ALS ZEITSCHRIFT FÜR EIN SPEZIELLES PUBLIKUM DARSTELLT. (USA)

▲ 112 PORTRAIT DE L'ARTISTE/DESIGNER/ ILLUSTRATEUR MILTON GLASER, PUBLIÉ DANS LE MAGAZINE *LEAR'S*. (USA)

▲ 113 D'UNE CAMPAGNE DE PUBLICITÉ DE *PC MAGAZINE*, METTANT EN RELIEF LE CARAC-TÈRE UNIQUE DE CETTE REVUE, DESTINÉE À UN PUBLIC SPÉCIALISÉ. (USA)

PHOTOGRAPHER:
MARY ELLEN MARK
REPRESENTATIVE:
FALKLAND ROAD, INC.
PUBLISHER:
ROLLING STONE
ART DIRECTOR:
FRED WOODWARD
PHOTO EDITOR:
LAURIE KRATOCHVIL
114

PHOTOGRAPHER:
HERB RITTS
PUBLISHERS:
INTERVIEW, PHOTO
> 115

■ 114 BLIND CHILDREN PICKING FLOWERS, A PHOTO TAKEN AT A SPECIAL SCHOOL IN KIEV, UKRAINE. IT APPEARED IN AN ARTICLE ON PHOTOGRAPHER MARY ELLEN MARK IN *ROLLING STONE* AS WELL AS IN THE BOOK "MARY ELLEN MARK, 25 YEARS." (USA)

● 114 BLINDE KINDER EINER SONDERSCHULE IN KIEW, UKRAINE, BEIM BLUMENPFLÜCKEN. DIE AUFNAHME ERSCHIEN IN EINEM ARTIKEL ÜBER MARY ELLEN MARK IN DER ZEITSCHRIFT *ROLLING STONE* SOWIE IN DEM BUCH «MARY ELLEN MARK, 25 YEARS». (USA)

▲ 114 ENFANTS D'UNE ÉCOLE POUR AVEUGLES À KIEV, EN UKRAINE. L'UNE DES PHOTOS DE MARY ELLEN MARK PUBLIÉES DANS LE MAGAZINE *ROLLING STONE* ET TIRÉES DU LIVRE: «MARY ELLEN MARK, 25 ANS DE PHOTOGRAPHIE». (USA)

■ 115 PORTRAIT OF MADONNA WHICH APPEARED WITH PHOTOS FROM HER BANNED CLIP IN A SPECIAL ISSUE ON ROCK STARS OF FRENCH MAGAZINE *PHOTO*. (FRA)

● 115 PORTRÄT VON MADONNA, DAS ZUSAMMEN MIT AUFNAHMEN IHRES VERBOTENEN CLIPS IN EINER NUMMER DES MAGAZINS *PHOTO* ÜBER ROCKSTARS. (FRA)

▲ 115 PORTRAIT DE MADONNA PARU DANS UN NUMÉRO DU MAGAZINE *PHOTO* DANS LEQUEL FURENT PUBLIÉES LES PHOTOS DU CLIP INTERDIT DE LA CHANTEUSE. (FRA)

PHOTOGRAPHER:
PATRICK DEMARCHELIER
PUBLISHER:
PHOTO
< 116

PHOTOGRAPHER:
MICHAEL O'BRIEN
REPRESENTATIVE:
MICHAEL ASH
CAMERA:
HASSELBLAD
FILM:
KODAK EPP
PUBLISHER:
LIFE
ART DIRECTOR:
MIMI PARK
PICTURE EDITOR:
BARBARA BAKER
BURROWS
117

PHOTOGRAPHER:
MICHAEL O'BRIEN
REPRESENTATIVE:
MICHAEL ASH
CAMERA:
HASSELBLAD
FILM:
FUJI RDP
PUBLISHER:
NATIONAL GEOGRAPHIC
PHOTOGRAPHY DIRECTOR:
THOMAS R. KENNEDY
PICTURE EDITOR:
MARY G. SMITH
STYLIST:
KATE BERGH
118

■ 116 PORTRAIT OF MADONNA ON THE COVER OF FRENCH MAGAZINE *PHOTO*. (FRA)

■ 117 WINSTON ROCHE, 92, WHO SERVED IN THE US ARMY DURING WORLD WAR I, PHOTOGRAPHED FOR A SERIES ON WAR VETERANS, ASSIGNED BY *LIFE* MAGAZINE. (USA)

■ 118 ROOSEVELT THOMAS WILLIAMS, 87-YEAR-OLD BARRELHOUSE BLUES MUSICIAN, KNOWN AS THE GREY GHOST, WHO USED TO TRAVEL BY FREIGHT TRAIN PLAYING FROM TOWN TO TOWN. HE WAS PORTRAYED FOR A FEATURE IN *NATIONAL GEOGRAPHIC* MAGAZINE WHO WANTED A CROSS SECTION OF THE CITIZENS OF AUSTIN, TEXAS. (USA)

● 116 PORTRÄT VON MADONNA, DAS AUF DEM UMSCHLAG VON PHOTO ERSCHIEN.(FRA)

● 117 EIN 92JÄHRIGER VETERAN, DER ALS LEUTNANT FÜR DIE USA IM ERSTEN WELTKRIEG KÄMPFTE. AUS EINER PORTRÄTREIHE VON KRIEGSVETERANEN FÜR *LIFE*. (USA)

● 118 ROOSEVELT THOMAS WILLIAMS, 87 JAHRE ALT UND BLUES-MUSIKER. FRÜHER REISTE ER FÜR SEINE AUFTRITTE MIT GÜTERZÜGEN VON STADT ZU STADT. DAS MAGAZIN *NATIONAL GEOGRAPHIC* HATTE DEN PHOTOGRAPHEN BEAUFTRAGT, PORTRÄTS EINES QUERSCHNITTS DER BÜRGER VON AUSTIN, TEXAS, ZU MACHEN. (USA)

▲ 116 PORTRAIT DE MADONNA PARU EN COUVERTURE DU MAGAZINE *PHOTO*. (FRA)

▲ 117 D'UNE SÉRIE SUR LES VÉTÉRANS DE L'ARMÉE AMÉRICAINE, POUR *LIFE*. WINSTON ROCHE, 92 ANS, QUI SERVIT LORS DE LA PREMIÈRE GUERRE MONDIALE. (USA)

▲ 118 D'UNE SÉRIE SUR LES HABITANTS DE LA VILLE D'AUSTIN, RÉALISÉE POUR LE MAGAZINE *NATIONAL GEOGRAPHIC*. ICI, ROOSEVELT THOMAS WILLIAMS, 87 ANS, MUSICIEN DE BLUES, QUI SE DÉPLAÇAIT DE VILLE EN VILLE DANS DES WAGONS DE MARCHANDISES, APPARAISSANT ET DISPARAISSANT «TEL UN FANTÔME». (USA)

PHOTOGRAPHER:
SHEILA METZNER
CAMERA: NIKON
FILM: POLAROID 35MM
PUBLISHERS:
NEW YORK TIMES (119)
VOGUE PARIS (120)
VOGUE ITALIA (121)

ART DIRECTORS:
JANET FROELICH (119)
MARY SHANAHAN (120)
FABIEN BARON (121)
119-121

■ 119-121 "RICK, STELLA, AND JOSIE," A POR-
TRAIT SERIES. STELLA WAS ASLEEP ON THE
ROCKY BEACH ADJACENT TO THE PHOTOG-
RAPHER'S HOUSE. SHE WAS UNAWARE THAT
SHE WAS BEING PHOTOGRAPHED. (USA)

● 119-121 «RICK, STELLA UND JOSIE», POR-
TRÄTREIHE. STELLA SCHLIEF AM STRAND IN
DER NÄHE DES HAUSES DER PHOTOGRAPHIN
SHEILA METZNER. SIE MERKTE NICHT, DASS
SIE PHOTOGRAPHIERT WURDE. (USA)

▲ 119-121 «RICK, STELLA ET JOSIE». STELLA
DORMAIT SUR UNE PLAGE PROCHE DE LA MAI-
SON DE LA PHOTOGRAPHE SHEILA METZNER.
ELLE N'A PAS REMARQUÉ QU'ON LA PHO-
TOGRAPHIAIT. (USA)

PHOTOGRAPHER:
GILLES LARRAIN
CAMERA:
ROLLEIFLEX SL 66E
PHOTO MONTAGE,
COLLAGE AND PAINTING:
COCO LARRAIN,
GILLES LARRAIN

CLIENT:
THE MEADOWS MUSEUM
ART DIRECTORS:
ARTHUR EISENBERG,
SAUL TORRES
AGENCY:
EISENBERG & ASSOC.
122

■ 122 A GALLERY OF PORTRAITS OF CELEBRITIES PRESENTED IN A CATALOG FOR AN EXHIBITION OF PHOTOGRAPHER GILLES LARRAIN AT THE MEADOWS MUSEUM. THE PHOTOS WERE MOUNTED ON A WOOD PANEL AND FIXED WITH A BEESWAX COMPOSITE. (USA)

● 122 PORTRÄTS VON BERÜHMTHEITEN AUS DEM KATALOG FÜR EINE AUSSTELLUNG DES PHOTOGRAPHEN GILLES LARRAIN IN DALLAS. DIE AUFNAHMEN WURDEN AUF HOLZ AUFGEZOGEN UND MIT EINER BIENENWACHSMISCHUNG FIXIERT. (USA)

▲ 122 PORTRAITS DE CÉLÉBRITÉS FIGURANT DANS LE CATALOGUE D'UNE EXPOSITION DU PHOTOGRAPHE GILLES LARRAIN AU MEADOWS MUSEUM DE DALLAS. LES PHOTOS ONT ÉTÉ MONTÉES SUR BOIS ET FIXÉES AVEC UN MÉLANGE À BASE DE CIRE D'ABEILLES. (USA)

PHOTOGRAPHER:
MICHAEL O'BRIEN
REPRESENTATIVE:
MICHAEL ASH
CAMERA:
HASSELBLAD
FILM:
FUJI RDP
PUBLISHER:
NATIONAL GEOGRAPHIC
PHOTOGRAPHY DIRECTOR:
THOMAS R. KENNEDY
PICTURE EDITOR:
MARY G. SMITH
123

PHOTOGRAPHER:
MARK SELIGER
CAMERA:
HASSELBLAD
FILM:
FUJI
PUBLISHER:
ROLLING STONE
ART DIRECTOR:
FRED WOODWARD
PHOTO EDITOR:
LAURIE
KRATOCHVIL
124

■ 123 PORTRAIT OF SINGER AND SONGWRITER WILLIE NELSON, TAKEN ON HIS RANCH NEAR AUSTIN. THE IMAGE IS PART OF A SERIES ON THE CITIZENS OF AUSTIN, COMMISSIONED BY *NATIONAL GEOGRAPHIC* MAGAZINE. (USA)

■ 124 PORTRAIT OF SLASH FOR A COVER STORY IN *ROLLING STONE* MAGAZINE. THE PHOTOGRAPH WAS TAKEN AT SLASH'S HOME IN HIS BACKYARD. (USA)

■ 125 COAL CARRIERS IN SCHWERIN, PHOTO-GRAPHED WITH NATURAL LIGHT ON NEGATIVE FILM WITH AN 8X10 INCH CAMERA. PHOTO-GRAPH FROM A PORTRAIT SERIES OF LABOR-ERS, WOMEN, AND CHILDREN IN EAST GER-MANY AFTER THE FALL OF THE WALL. (GER)

● 123 DER SÄNGER UND SONGWRITER WILLIE NELSON, AUFGENOMMEN AUF SEINER RANCH. DIE AUFNAHME GEHÖRT ZU EINER PORTRÄT-REIHE VON BÜRGERN DER STADT AUSTIN, FÜR DAS MAGAZIN *NATIONAL GEOGRAPHIC*. (USA)

● 124 PORTRÄT DES SÄNGERS SLASH, MIT-GLIED DER GRUPPE GUNS N' ROSES, FÜR EI-NEN BEITRAG IN DER AMERIKANISCHEN ZEIT-SCHRIFT *ROLLING STONE*. (USA)

● 125 KOHLENSCHLEPPER IN SCHWERIN, BEI TAGESLICHT AUF NEGATIVMATERIAL MIT 8X10 INCH-KAMERA PHOTOGRAPHIERT. DIE AUF-NAHME GEHÖRT ZU EINER PORTRÄTREIHE VON MENSCHEN IM OSTEN DEUTSCHLANDS NACH DER ÖFFNUNG DER MAUER. (GER)

▲ 123 D'UNE SÉRIE SUR LES HABITANTS D'AUSTIN, POUR *NATIONAL GEOGRAPHIC*. ICI, LE PORTRAIT DE L'AUTEUR-INTERPRÈTE WILLIE NELSON, PRIS DANS SON RANCH DES ENVIRONS D'AUSTIN. (USA)

▲ 124 PORTRAIT DE SLASH, MEMBRE DU GROUPE ROCK GUNS N' ROSES, PUBLIÉE EN COUVERTURE D'UN NUMÉRO DE *ROLLING STONE*. (USA)

▲ 125 HERCHEURS DES MINES DE SCHWERIN, PHOTOGRAPHIÉS SOUS UN ÉCLAIRAGE NATU-REL SUR NÉGATIF AVEC UN APPAREIL 8X10 INCH. D'UNE SÉRIE DE PORTRAITS, RÉALISÉS EN ALLEMAGNE DE L'EST, APRÈS L'OUVER-TURE DU MUR. (GER)

PHOTOGRAPHER:

EBERHARD GRAMES

CAMERA:

8 X 10

PUBLISHER:

DRUCKEREI BRILLANT

OFFSET

ART DIRECTOR:

EBERHARD GRAMES

DESIGNER:

EBERHARD GRAMES

125

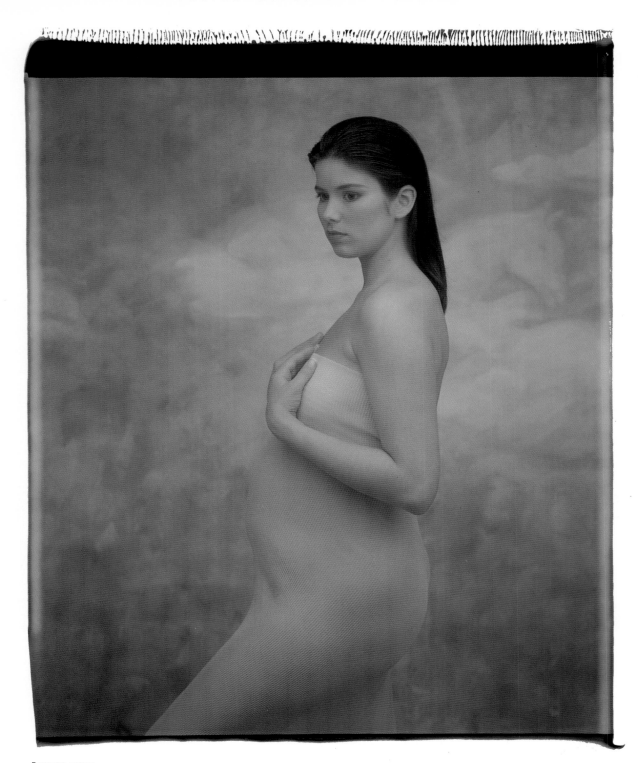

PHOTOGRAPH:

JOYCE TENNESON

CAMERA:

POLAROID 20X24

FILM:

POLACOLOR 20X24

PUBLISHER:

PARENTING

ART DIRECTOR:

DIAN AZIZA OOKA

DESIGNER:

DIAN AZIZA OOKA

STYLIST:

DEBRA PINTER

HAIR, MAKEUP:

KELLY QUAN

126

PHOTOGRAPHER:
JOHN KOLESA
CAMERA:
SINAR P2 4X5
FILM:
POLAROID 55
127

■ **126** THIS PHOTOGRAPH ILLUSTRATED AN ARTICLE IN *PARENTING* MAGAZINE ON BREAST CANCER WHICH IS BEING DIAGNOSED IN AN INCREASING NUMBER OF YOUNG MOTHERS. A SOFT BOX FROM THE CEILING AND TWO ON THE FLOOR WERE USED TO PRODUCE EVEN, FLAT LIGHT. (USA)

■ **127** TWO FROM A SELF-ASSIGNED SERIES OF VERY CLOSE AND PERSONAL PORTRAITS. THE EDGES ARE AN IMPORTANT ELEMENT, FRAMED AND ACCENTUATED BY THE BORDERS OF THE POLAROID FILM. (USA)

● **126** DIE AUFNAHME ILLUSTRIERTE EINEN BEITRAG IM MAGAZIN *PARENTING* ÜBER BRUSTKREBS, DER IN ZUNEHMENDEM MASSE AUCH BEI JUNGEN MÜTTERN FESTGESTELLT WIRD. EINE SOFTBOX AN DER DECKE UND ZWEI AUF DEM BODEN SORGTEN FÜR GLEICH-MÄSSIGES, GEDÄMPFTES LICHT. (USA)

● **127** ZWEI PORTRÄTS AUS EINER FREIEN SERIE SEHR PERSÖNLICHER PORTRÄTS. DIE RÄNDER DER AUFNAHMEN SIND EIN WICH-TIGES ELEMENT, DAS VOM POLAROIDFILM NOCH HERVORGEHOBEN WIRD. (USA)

▲ **126** CETTE PHOTO ILLUSTRAIT UN ARTICLE DU MAGAZINE *PARENTING* SUR LE CANCER DU SEIN, QUI ATTEINT TOUJOURS UN PLUS GRAND NOMBRE DE JEUNES MÈRES. LA LU-MIÈRE RÉGULIÈRE A ÉTÉ OBTENUE À L'AIDE D'UNE SOFTBOX AU PLAFOND ET DE DEUX SUR LE SOL. (USA)

▲ **127** DEUX PORTRAITS TIRÉS D'UNE SÉRIE D'ÉTUDES PERSONNELLES. LES ENCADRE-MENTS, QUI SONT ENCORE MIS EN VALEUR PAR LA BORDURE DU FILM POLAROÏD, JOUENT UN RÔLE ESSENTIEL. (USA)

PHOTOGRAPHER:
RAYMOND DEPARDON
REPRESENTATIVE:
KIM DOAN/
MAGNUM PHOTOS
CLIENT:
MAISON DES JEUNES
ET DE LA CULTURE DE
VALENCE
ART DIRECTOR:
CATHERINE GADON
DESIGNERS:
PASCAL CHALLIER,
LAURENCE FONTAINE
128

PHOTOGRAPHER:
ELIZABETH ZESCHIN
CAMERA:
NIKON
129

PHOTOGRAPHER:
TIMOTHY GREENFIELD-
SANDERS
REPRESENTATIVE:
STOCKLAND/MARTEL
CAMERA:
POLAROID 20X24
> 130

■ 128 "THURSDAY, 11TH JANUARY 1990, BARTHELEMY FOUNDRY CREST." PHOTOGRAPH FROM A CATALOG FOR AN EXHIBITION ON "ART AND INDUSTRY IN MOVEMENT" IN THE MUSEUM OF VALENCE. (FRA)

■ 129 "YASHINA KAMAL, NEW YORK CITY, 1991", PORTRAIT TAKEN WITH DAYLIGHT IN THE PHOTOGRAPHER'S STUDIO. (USA)

■ 130 "PORTRAIT OF WILLIAM WEGMAN WITH FAY." THIS POLAROID SHOT OF WEGMAN WHO IS FAMOUS FOR HIS PORTRAITS OF DOGS, WAS SHOWN IN A ONE-MAN EXHIBITION OF PHOTOGRAPHER TIMOTHY GREENFIELD SANDERS. WHO WOULD DENY THE RESEMBLANCE OF MASTER AND ANIMAL? (USA)

● 128 «DONNERSTAG, 11. JANUAR 1990, GIESSEREI BARTHELEMY CREST.» DIESE AUFNAHME STAMMT AUS DEM KATALOG ZUR AUSSTELLUNG «KUNST UND INDUSTRIE IN BEWEGUNG» IM MUSEUM VON VALENCE. (FRA)

● 129 «YAHSINA KAMAL, NEW YORK CITY, 1991.» EIN IM STUDIO MIT TAGESLICHT AUFGENOMMENES PORTRÄT. (USA)

● 130 WER WÜRDE EINE GEWISSE ÄHNLICHKEIT ZWISCHEN HUND UND SEINEM HERRN LEUGNEN? PORTRÄT DES KÜNSTLERS WILLIAM WEGMAN MIT SEINEM HUND FAY. DIESE POLAROID-AUFNAHME WURDE IN EINER EINZELAUSSTELLUNG DES PHOTOGRAPHEN TIMOTHY GREENFIELD-SANDERS GEZEIGT. (USA)

▲ 128 «JEUDI 11 JANVIER 1990. FONDERIE BARTHÉLÉMY CREST». LA PHOTO DE LA SÉRIE «INTIMITÉS INDUSTRIELLES» EST TIRÉE DU CATALOGUE DE L'EXPOSITION «ART ET INDUSTRIE EN MOUVEMENT» À VALENCE. (FRA)

▲ 129 PORTRAIT DE YASMINA KAMAL, RÉALISÉ DANS L'APPARTEMENT NEW-YORKAIS DE LA PHOTOGRAPHE. (USA)

▲ 130 ON NE SAURAIT NIER UNE CERTAINE RESSEMBLANCE ENTRE UN CHIEN ET SON MAÎTRE. PORTRAIT DE WILLIAM WEGMAN AVEC FAY, SON CHIEN ET MODÈLE PRÉFÉRÉ. CETTE PHOTO POLAROÏD A ÉTÉ PRÉSENTÉE DANS UNE EXPOSITION DU PHOTOGRAPHE TIMOTHY GREENFIELD-SANDERS. (USA)

PHOTOGRAPHER:
ANIA WALISIEWICZ
REPRESENTATIVE:
CAROL ACEY

131

PHOTOGRAPHER:

TIMOTHY GREENFIELD-
SANDERS

REPRESENTATIVE:

STOCKLAND/MARTEL

CAMERA:

POLAROID 20X24

132

■ 131 THE BROTHER OF THE PHOTOGRAPHER POSING AS ROACH. (GBR)

■ 132 WHILE SHOOTING INDIVIDUAL PORTRAITS OF "ARTISTS WHO USE PHOTOGRAPHY IN THEIR WORK AND WHO ARE NOT PHOTOGRAPHERS", THE PHOTOGRAPHER MADE THIS "CONNECTING GROUP PORTRAIT" IN THE FEW MOMENTS OF OVERLAP TIME BETWEEN THE SCHEDULED PORTRAIT SESSIONS. HE TOOK ONLY ONE EXPOSURE ON THE 20X24 POLAROID CAMERA OF THE DEPARTING AND NEWLY ARRIVING ARTIST TOGETHER. (USA)

● 131 DER BRUDER DER PHOTOGRAPHIN, EINE KÜCHENSCHABE DARSTELLEND. (GBR)

● 132 ALS DER PHOTOGRAPH EINZELPORTRÄTS VON KÜNSTLERN MACHTE, DIE PHOTOGRAPHIE VERWENDEN, ABER KEINE PHOTOGRAPHEN SIND, NUTZTE ER DIE KURZEN MOMENTE ZWISCHEN DEN TERMINEN, UM DIESE GRUPPENPORTRÄTS ZU MACHEN, AUF DENEN JEWEILS DIE KOMMENDEN UND GEHENDEN PERSONEN ZU SEHEN SIND. ER ARBEITETE MIT EINER EINZIGEN EINSTELLUNG MIT EINER POLAROID-KAMERA 20X24. (USA)

▲ 131 LE FRÈRE DE LA PHOTOGRAPHE A IMITÉ ICI UN CANCRELAT. (GBR)

▲ 132 ALORS QUE LE PHOTOGRAPHE RÉALISAIT UNE SÉRIE DE PORTRAITS D'ARTISTES QUI UTILISENT LA PHOTOGRAPHIE SANS ÊTRE DES PHOTOGRAPHES PROFESSIONNELS, IL PROFITA DES COURTS MOMENTS DE RÉPIT ENTRE LES RENDEZ-VOUS POUR FAIRE CES PORTRAITS DE GROUPE: ON Y VOIT LES PERSONNES QUI ENTRENT ET QUI SORTENT. IL A OPÉRÉ AVEC UNE SEULE EXPOSITION, UTILISANT UN POLAROÏD 20X24. (USA)

PHOTOGRAPHER:
CHRYSANTHA
CAMERA:
TOYO 9X12
133, 134

PHOTOGRAPHER:
YURI DOJC
REPRESENTATIVES:
FRAN BLACK/THE
ARTS COUNSEL (USA),
HUGO MAYER
NORTEN (GER),
VAN NETOFF (CAN)
CAMERA:
NIKON
FILM:
KODAK INFRA-RED
ART DIRECTOR:
YURI DOJC
> 135

■ **133, 134** THESE TWO PHOTOGRAPHS ENTI-
TLED "PORTRAIT OF CHARLOTTE" ARE PART
OF A PORTRAIT SERIES FOR AN EXHIBITION.
THE PHOTOGRAPHER PRODUCED THE NEGA-
TIVE MATERIAL HERSELF; PRINT: GELANTINE
SILVER 25X33.5 CM. (GER)

■ **135** THIS STUDIO PHOTOGRAPH ON KODAK
INFRA-RED FILM IS PART OF A SERIES OF
NUDES FOR A BOOK. THE COLLIE IS MADE OF
PLASTER. PHOTOGRAPHER YURI DOJC IS
KNOWN FOR JUXTAPOSING ALL KINDS OF
CREATURES IN UNEXPECTED WAYS. (CAN)

● **133, 134** DIE BEIDEN AUFNAHMEN MIT DEM
TITEL «PORTRÄT CHARLOTTE» ENTSTANDEN
INNERHALB EINES PORTRÄT-ZYKLUS FÜR EINE
AUSSTELLUNG DER PHOTOGRAPHIN. DAS NE-
GATIVMATERIAL STELLTE SIE SELBST HER;
ABZUG: GELANTINE SILBER 25X33,5CM. (GER)

● **135** DIESE STUDIOAUFNAHME GEHÖRT ZU
EINER REIHE VON AKTAUFNAHMEN FÜR EIN
BUCH. DER COLLIE IST AUS GIPS. YURI DOJC,
DER PHOTOGRAPH, IST FÜR EIGENARTIGE
GEGENÜBERSTELLUNGEN UND KOMPOSITIO-
NEN BEKANNT. (CAN)

▲ **133, 134** LES PHOTOS INTITULÉES «POR-
TRAIT DE CHARLOTTE» FONT PARTIE D'UN
CYCLE DE PORTRAITS, RÉALISÉS POUR UNE
EXPOSITION DE LA PHOTOGRAPHE. CELLE-CI
A PRÉPARÉ ELLE-MÊME SON NÉGATIF. TIRA-
GE: GELATINE ARGENT 25X33,5CM. (GER)

▲ ·**135** D'UNE SÉRIE DE PHOTOS DE NUS, DES
ÉTUDES PERSONNELLES RÉALISÉES POUR UN
LIVRE. CELLE-CI FUT RÉALISÉE EN STUDIO.
LE COLLEY EST EN PLÂTRE. YURI DOJC, LE
PHOTOGRAPHE, EST CONNU POUR SES JUXTA-
POSITIONS INATTENDUES. (CAN)

PHOTOGRAPHER:

SUE BENNETT

CAMERA:

NIKON

FILM:

KODACHROME 64

PUBLISHER:

POMEGRANATE

CALENDARS & BOOKS

DESIGNER:

BRIAN BLANCHARD

136

PHOTOGRAPHER:

TIM BIEBER

CLIENT:

ILLINOIS DEPARTMENT

OF TOURISM

ART DIRECTOR:

STEVE JULIUSSON

AGENCY:

MCCONNAUGHY, STEIN,

SCHMIDT & BROWN

STUDIO:

LISKA & ASSOCIATES

137

■ 136 FROM A SERIES FOR THE "1991 NATIVE AMERICAN CALENDAR," PHOTOGRAPHED WITH NATURAL LIGHT IN THE UNITED STATES AND CANADA. (USA)

■ 137 THE "BLACK LONE RANGER," FROM A SERIES ON CHICAGO NIGHTCLUBS. THE LONE RANGER IS A REGULAR CHARACTER IN CHECKERBOARD LOUNGE, A BLUES CLUB. (USA)

● 136 AUFNAHMEN AUS EINEM KALENDER ÜBER DIE UREINWOHNER AMERIKAS. SIE WURDEN BEI TAGESLICHT IN DEN USA UND KANADA AUFGENOMMEN. (USA)

● 137 DER «BLACK LONE RANGER» IST REGELMÄSSIGER GAST IN DER CHECKERBOARD LOUNGE, EINEM BLUES CLUB IN CHICAGO. AUFNAHME FÜR EIN TOURISTIKBÜRO. (USA)

▲ 136 PHOTOS D'UN CALENDRIER SUR LES PEUPLES AUTOCHTONES DE L'AMÉRIQUE. ELLES ONT ÉTÉ PRISES AUX USA ET AU CANADA, SOUS UN ÉCLAIRAGE NATUREL. (USA)

▲ 137 «BLACK LONE RANGER». IMAGE D'UNE SÉRIE SUR LES NIGHT-CLUBS DE CHICAGO. PORTRAIT D'UN HABITUÉ DU CHECKERBOARD LOUNGE, UN CLUB DE BLUES. (USA)

PHOTOGRAPHER:
SCOGIN MAYO
REPRESENTATIVE:
FRIEND AND JOHNSON
CAMERA:
ROLLEI 6006
FILM:
ILFORD HP5-PLUS
PUBLISHER:
MÄNNER VOGUE
ART DIRECTOR:
LESLEY VINSON
138

PHOTOGRAPHER:
SERGEJ KISCHNICK
CAMERA:
HASSELBLAD 150MM
FILM:
KODAK PLUS-X
PUBLISHER:
VOGUE
ART DIRECTOR:
ANGELICA BLECH-
SCHMIDT
STYLIST:
GOSHKA OSTROWSKA
139

PHOTOGRAPHER:
MARC NORBERG
CAMERA:
HASSELBLAD
FILM:
KODAK PLUS-X
CLIENT:
BLUES HEAVEN
FOUNDATION
ART DIRECTOR:
MARC NORBERG
DESIGNER:
MICHAEL SKEJEI
140

PHOTOGRAPHER: ART DIRECTOR:
STEVE MARSEL   BOB MANLEY
CAMERA: DESIGNER:
SINAR F+ 4X5   BRENT CROXTON
FILM: AGENCY:
KODAK 100 PLUS   ALTMAN & MANLEY/
PUBLISHER: EAGLE ADVERTISING
BITSTREAM INC.   141

■ 138 PORTRAIT OF STERLING MORRISSON, FORMER MEMBER OF THE POP GROUP VELVET UNDERGROUND, FOR A PROFILE IN *MÄNNER VOGUE*. THE ONLY STIPULATION WAS THAT HE HAD TO BE PHOTOGRAPHED IN THE CONTEXT OF HIS CURRENT OCCUPATION AS A TUGBOAT CAPTAIN IN THE SHIP CHANNELS OF HOUSTON, TEXAS. (GER)

■ 139 PORTRAIT OF POLISH AUTHOR AND FILM DIRECTOR ZBIGNIEW TCZINSKI FOR THE GERMAN EDITION OF *VOGUE*. SHOT IN THE STUDIO WITH KODAK PLUS X FILM. (GER)

■ 140 THE PORTRAIT OF MUSICIAN ALBERT COLLINS FOR A LIMITED EDITION PORTFOLIO TO BENEFIT THE BLUES HEAVEN FOUNDATION, A NON-PROFIT ORGANIZATION. (USA)

■ 141 THE IDEA WAS TO SHOW THE EXPANDABLE FONT CARTRIDGE FOR LASER JET PRINTERS WITH PEOPLE IN PROVOCATIVE ENVIRONMENTS. THIS EIGHT FOOT HIGH MODEL OF THE CARTRIDGE WAS BUILT OUT OF FOAM. THE PRIMARY LIGHT WAS STROBE, DIFFUSED THROUGH A SOFT BOX. (USA)

● 138 PORTRÄT VON STERLING MORRISSON, DEM EHEMALIGEN MITGLIED DER POP-GRUPPE VELVET UNDERGROUND, FÜR EINEN BERICHT IN *MÄNNER VOGUE*. DIE EINZIGE VORGABE WAR, DASS DIE AUFNAHME EINEN BEZUG ZU SEINER JETZIGEN TÄTIGKEIT ALS KAPITÄN EINES SCHLEPPERS IN DEN KANÄLEN VON HOUSTON, TEXAS, HABEN MUSSTE (GER)

● 139 PORTRÄT DES POLNISCHEN AUTORS UND REGISSEURS ZBIGNIEW TCZINSKI FÜR DIE DEUTSCHE *VOGUE*. STUDIOAUFNAHME MIT KODAK PLUS X FILM. (GER)

● 140 PORTRÄT DES MUSIKERS ALBERT COLLINS FÜR EINE PHOTOMAPPE IN LIMITIERTER AUFLAGE ZUGUNSTEN DER STIFTUNG BLUES HEAVEN. (USA)

● 141 STATT EINER EINFACHEN PRODUKTAUFNAHME WURDEN ERWEITERBARE SCHRIFTKASSETTEN FÜR LASER-JET-DRUCKER MIT LEUTEN IN SPEZIELLER UMGEBUNG GEZEIGT. DIESES 2,5 METER HOHE MODELL BESTEHT AUS SCHAUMSTOFF. DAS STROBOSKOPLICHT WURDE MIT EINER SOFTBOX GESTREUT. (USA)

▲ 138 PORTRAIT DE STERLING MORRISSON, ANCIEN MEMBRE DU GROUPE CULTE DE LA FIN DES ANNÉES 60, LE VELVET UNDERGROUND, PUBLIÉ DANS *MÄNNER VOGUE*. IL A ÉTÉ PHOTOGRAPHIÉ, À LA DEMANDE DU MAGAZINE, DANS SON OCCUPATION ACTUELLE DE CAPITAINE D'UN REMORQUEUR DANS LE PORT D'HOUSTON, AU TEXAS. (GER)

▲ 139 PORTRAIT DE ZBIGNIEW TCZINSKI, UN AUTEUR ET METTEUR EN SCÈNE POLONAIS, POUR L'ÉDITION ALLEMANDE DE *VOGUE*. PHOTO PRISE EN STUDIO. (GER)

▲ 140 LE MUSICIEN ALBERT COLLINS. D'UNE SÉRIE DE PHOTOS RÉALISÉES POUR BLUES HEAVEN FOUNDATION, UNE ORGANISATION À BUT NON LUCRATIF. (USA)

▲ 141 LES CASSETTES DE CARACTÈRES POUR IMPRIMANTE À JET LASER SONT PRÉSENTÉES DANS UN CADRE SPÉCIAL, AVEC DES GENS INTÉRESSANTS. LA MAQUETTE EST EN MOUSSE. LE PHOTOGRAPHE A UTILISÉ UNE LUMIÈRE DE FLASH STROBOSCOPIQUE, DISSÉMINÉE PAR UNE SOFT BOX. (USA)

PHOTOGRAPHER:
DAVID PERRY
LAWRENCE
CAMERA:
NIKON F4
FILM:
FUJI CHROME 100D
142

PHOTOGRAPHER:
GERALD BYBEE
REPRESENTATIVE:
BYBEE STUDIOS
CAMERA:
ROLLEI SLX 21/4
FILM:
EPR EKTACHROME
64120
DESIGNER:
JENNIFER MORLA
DESIGN
143

PHOTOGRAPHER:
MARK SELIGER
CAMERA:
TOYO 4X5
FILM:
TRI-X 4X5
PUBLISHER:
ROLLING STONE
ART DIRECTOR:
FRED WOODWARD
PHOTO EDITOR:
LAURIE KRATOCHVIL
> 144

■ **142** PHOTOGRAPH FROM A SELF-PROMO-TIONAL SERIES SHOWING THE PHOTOGRA-PHER'S ABILITY TO PAINT WITH LIGHT EQUIP-MENT. SHOWN IS A LOCAL JUGGLER WITH A PAINTED CANVAS IN THE BACKGROUND. (USA)

■ **143** "MARISA." THIS PHOTOGRAPH ON EPR EKTACHROME 64120, WAS USED AS SELF-PRO-MOTION BY A PHOTO STUDIO STRIVING FOR A CONTEMPORARY LOOK. (USA)

■ **144** FROM AN UNPUBLISHED SERIES OF PORTRAITS OF BLUES MUSICIAN JOHN LEE HOOKER COMMISSIONED BY *ROLLING STONE*. THE PHOTOGRAPHER WANTED THESE POR-TRAITS TO BE SERIOUS, STRAIGHTFORWARD AND RESPECTFUL, SHOWING HIS APPRECIA-TION FOR MUSICIANS. (USA)

● **142** PORTRÄT EINES JONGLEURS ALS EI-GENWERBUNG DES PHOTOGRAPHEN, DER SEI-NE FÄHIGKEIT MIT LICHT ZU «MALEN» UNTER BEWEIS STELLEN WILL. DER HINTERGRUND IST EINE BEMALTE LEINWAND. (USA)

● **143** «MARISA». DIESE AUFNAHME WURDE ALS EIGENWERBUNG EINES PHOTOSTUDIOS VERWENDET, DAS EIN ZEITGEMÄSSES IMAGE WOLLTE. (USA)

● **144** AUS EINER REIHE UNVERÖFFENTLICHER PORTRÄTS DES BLUES-MUSIKERS JOHN LEE HOOKER, DIE VON *ROLLING STONE* IN AUF-TRAG GEGEBEN WURDEN. DER PHOTOGRAPH WOLLTE ERNSTE, EHRLICHE UND RESPEKT-VOLLE PORTRÄTS DER MUSIKER, UM SEINE ACHTUNG VOR IHNEN AUSDRÜCKEN. (USA)

▲ **142** PHOTO D'UNE SÉRIE AUTOPROMOTION-NELLE ILLUSTRANT LA FACULTÉ DU PHOTO-GRAPHE DE PEINDRE AVEC LA LUMIÈRE. ICI, LE PORTRAIT D'UN JONGLEUR LOCAL, DEVANT UNE TOILE DE FOND PEINTE. (USA)

▲ **143** «MARISA». CETTE PHOTO SERT DE PUB-LICITÉ À UN STUDIO DE PHOTOGRAPHE: L'IDÉE ÉTAIT DE SUGGÉRER LE CARACTÈRE CONTEMPORAIN DE CE STUDIO. (USA)

▲ **144** UN EXEMPLE D'UNE SÉRIE DE POR-TRAITS INÉDITS REPRÉSENTANT LE MUSICIEN DE BLUES JOHN LEE HOOKER, POUR *ROLLING STONE*. LE PHOTOGRAPHE VOULAIT FAIRE DES PORTRAITS SÉRIEUX, AUTHENTIQUES ET RESPECTABLES DES MUSICIENS, EXPRIMANT SON ADMIRATION POUR EUX. (USA)

PHOTOGRAPHER:
FRANK OCKENFELS 3
REPRESENTATIVE:
OUTLINE PRESS
PUBLISHER:
VANITY FAIR
HAIR, MAKEUP:
RASSCALE LEWIS
145

PHOTOGRAPHER:
FRANK W.
OCKENFELS 3
REPRESENTATIVE:
OUTLINE PRESS
PUBLISHER:
CREEM
> 146

■ 145 "QUEEN LATIFAH," FOR A SERIES ON FEMALE RAP ARTISTS IN *VANITY FAIR*. THE PHOTOGRAPHER AND RASSCALE LEWIS, THE HAIR AND MAKE-UP STYLIST, TRIED OUT VARIOUS PIECES OF JEWELRY AND FABRIC. THE CROWN IS ACTUALLY A NECKLACE WHICH HELD THE FABRIC IN PLACE. A NATURAL RAY OF LIGHT FROM A SKYLIGHT CAME AT JUST THE RIGHT MOMENT. (USA)

● 145 «QUEEN LATIFAH», PORTRÄT FÜR EINE REIHE ÜBER RAPERINNEN IN DER ZEITSCHRIFT *VANITY FAIR*. DER PHOTOGRAPH UND DIE MAKE-UP UND HAAR-STYLISTIN RASSCALE LEWIS, PROBIERTEN SCHMUCK UND STOFF – DIE KRONE IST EIGENTLICH EIN HALSSCHMUCK, DER HIER DEN STOFF HÄLT. EIN STRAHL NATÜRLICHEN LICHTES FIEL IM RICHTIGEN MOMENT VON OBEN EIN. (USA)

▲ 145 «QUEEN LATIFAH». PORTRAIT D'UNE SÉRIE SUR LES VEDETTES FÉMININES DU RAP, PARUE DANS *VANITY FAIR*. LE PHOTOGRAPHE ET LE MAQUILLEUR-COIFFEUR-STYLISTE RASSCALE LEWIS S'AMUSÈRENT À L'ORNER DE BIJOUX ET D'ÉTOFFES. LA COURONNE EST EN RÉALITÉ UN COLLIER: CE DERNIER MAINTIENT L'ÉTOFFE EN PLACE. UN RAYON DE LUMIÈRE TOMBAIT JUSTE SUR LA CHANTEUSE. (USA)

■ 146 PHOTOGRAPH FROM A SERIES FOR AN INTERVIEW WITH ROCK MUSICIAN ELVIS COSTELLO IN *CREEM* MAGAZINE. THIS PHOTOGRAPH WAS TAKEN IN A PARK NEAR ELVIS' HOME IN LONDON IN A RAIN STORM. (USA)

● 146 AUFNAHME AUS EINEM INTERVIEW MIT DEM ROCKMUSIKER ELVIS COSTELLO IN DER ZEITSCHRIFT *CREEM*. SIE WURDE BEI STURM UND REGEN IN EINEM PARK IN LONDON IN DER NÄHE VON ELVIS' WOHNUNG GEMACHT. (USA)

▲ 146 PORTRAIT DU MUSICIEN ROCK ELVIS COSTELLO POUR LE MAGAZINE *CREEM*. LA PHOTO FUT RÉALISÉE EN PLEINE TEMPÊTE ET SOUS LA PLUIE DANS UN PARC DE LONDRES, PROCHE DE SON APPARTEMENT. (USA)

PHOTOGRAPHER: PUBLISHER:
EBERHARD GRAMES   DRUCKEREI BRILLANT
CAMERA: OFFSET
8X10   ART DIRECTOR:
                      EBERHARD GRAMES
                      147

■ 147 A TRUCK DRIVER FROM MEISSEN. THIS PHOTOGRAPH WAS TAKEN IN DAYLIGHT AND IS PART OF A PORTRAIT SERIES OF LABORERS, WOMAN AND CHILDREN IN EAST GERMANY AFTER THE DEMOLITION OF THE WALL. (GER)

● 147 EIN LASTWAGENFAHRER AUS MEISSEN - PORTRÄT AUS EINER SERIE ÜBER MENSCHEN IM OSTEN DEUTSCHLANDS NACH ÖFFNUNG DER MAUER, BEI TAGESLICHT AUF NEGATIV-MATERIAL PHOTOGRAPHIERT. (GER)

▲ 147 UN CHAUFFEUR DE POIDS-LOURD DE MEISSEN. PORTRAIT TIRÉ D'UNE SÉRIE SUR LE PEUPLE EST-ALLEMAND APRÈS LA RÉUNI-FICATION. PHOTO SUR NÉGATIF, PRISE EN LUMIÈRE NATURELLE. (GER)

■ 148 "MAKING BREAD," PHOTOGRAPHED AT AL HUSSEIN CAMP, JORDAN, AND PUBLISHED IN A BOOK. (USA)

● 148 «BROTBACKEN», IN EINEM BUCH VER-ÖFFENTLICHTE AUFNAHME, DIE IM LAGER AL HUSSEIN, JORDANIEN, ENTSTAND. (USA)

▲ 148 «LA CUISSON DU PAIN». PHOTO PRISE DANS LE CAMP DE AL HUSSEIN, EN JORDANIE, ET PUBLIÉE DANS UN LIVRE. (USA)

■ 149 PORTRAIT IN *INDEPENDENT MAGAZINE* FOR A PROFILE ON AMERICAN JAZZ SINGER ELIZABETH WELCH. (GBR)

● 149 PORTRÄT DER AMERIKANISCHEN JAZZ-SÄNGERIN ELIZABETH WELCH, AUS EINEM ARTIKEL IM *INDEPENDENT MAGAZINE*. (GBR)

▲ 149 LA CHANTEUSE AMÉRICAINE DE JAZZ ELIZABETH WELCH, PHOTOGRAPHIÉE POUR *INDEPENDENT MAGAZINE*. (GBR)

(TOP)   DESIGNER: (BOTTOM)   PUBLISHER:

PHOTOGRAPHER: DAVID JENNY   PHOTOGRAPHER: *INDEPENDENT*

JOHN RUNNING   **148**   DAVID GAMBLE   *MAGAZINE*

PUBLISHER: CAMERA: PICTURE EDITOR:

NORTHLAND   MAMIYA 6X9   COLIN JACOBSON

PUBLISHING   **149**

PHOTOGRAPHER:
DIRK KARSTEN
REPRESENTATIVE:
ART PRODUCTIONTEAM
ART DIRECTOR:
DIRK KARSTEN
150

PHOTOGRAPHER:
MICHAEL BIONDO
CAMERA:
HASSELBLAD
FILM:
FUJI
PUBLISHER:
EGG MAGAZINE
ART DIRECTOR:
DOUGLESS RICCARDI
PHOTO EDITOR:
JIM FRANCO
151

PHOTOGRAPHER:
VOLKMANN
REPRESENTATIVE:
LIZ LI
CAMERA:
HASSELBLAD
PUBLISHER:
VOGUE ESPANA
ART DIRECTOR:
VOLKMANN
DESIGNER:
VOLKMANN
> 152

■ 150 PHOTOGRAPH OF A JAPANESE KENDO FIGHTER IN TRADITIONAL OUTFIT, THE IMAGE WAS USED FOR THE PHOTOGRAPHER'S SELF-PROMOTION. (NLD)

■ 151 A CHINESE HAT PHOTOGRAPHED BY MICHAEL BIONDO FOR A FEATURE ON FASHION DESIGNER MARY MCFADDEN. VARIOUS GELS AND FILTERS WERE USED. (USA)

■ 152 THIS PHOTOGRAPH WAS PART OF AN EDITORIAL ON MEN'S FITNESS AND GROOMING FOR *VOGUE* ESPANA. IT WAS TAKEN IN THE STUDIO WITH CALUMET SPOT STROBE RIGGED FOR SPEEDOTRON POWER PACKS. (SPA)

● 150 AUFNAHME EINES JAPANISCHEN KENDO-KÄMPFERS IN DER TRADITIONELLEN KAMPF-KLEIDUNG. DER PHOTOGRAPH VERWENDETE SIE ALS EIGENWERBUNG. (NLD)

● 151 EIN CHINESISCHER HUT, AUFGENOMMEN FÜR EINEN BEITRAG ÜBER DIE MODE-STYLI-STIN MARY MCFADDEN. VERSCHIEDENE GELS UND FILTER WURDEN VERWENDET. (USA)

● 152 DIESE AUFNAHME ERSCHIEN IN EINEM ARTIKEL IN DER SPANISCHEN *VOGUE* ÜBER FITNESS UND KÖRPERPFLEGE DER MÄNNER. SIE ENTSTAND IM STUDIO MIT STROBOSKOP-BLITZLICHT. (SPA)

▲ 150 PHOTO D'UN LUTTEUR ASIATIQUE DE KENDO, REVÊTU DU VÊTEMENT TRADITION-NEL, UTILISÉE COMME AUTOPROMOTION PAR LE PHOTOGRAPHE. (NLD)

▲ 151 UN CHAPEAU CHINOIS, PHOTOGRAPHIÉ POUR UN REPORTAGE DE MODE SUR LA STY-LISTE MARY MCFADDEN. DIVERS GELS ET FIL-TRES ONT ÉTÉ UTILISÉS. (USA)

▲ 152 PHOTO ILLUSTRANT UN ARTICLE SUR LA MISE EN FORME ET L'ENTRAÎNEMENT SPORTIF MASCULIN, PARU DANS L'ÉDITION ESPAGNOLE DE VOGUE. ELLE A ÉTÉ PRISE EN STUDIO AVEC LUMIÈRE STROBOSCOPIQUE. (SPA)

PRODUCTS

SACHAUFNAHMEN

PRODUITS

(FIRST PAGE OF
PRODUCT SECTION)
PHOTOGRAPHER:
STEFAN KIRCHNER
CLIENT:
ALESSI SPA
ART DIRECTOR:
CHRISTOPH RADL
DESIGNER:
PHILIPPE STARCK
AGENCY:
SOTTSASS ASSOCIATI
< 153

(THIS SPREAD)

PHOTOGRAPHER:

HANS HANSEN

ART DIRECTOR:

FRANZ EPPING

PUBLISHER:

SPORTS

GRUNER & JAHR

154, 155

■ **153** (FIRST PAGE OF PRODUCT SECTION) KETTLE DESIGNED BY PHILIPPE STARCK PHOTOGRAPHED FOR AN ALESSI BROCHURE. (ITA)

■ **154, 155** A HIGH-TECH GEAR OF THE NEW GENERATION AND AN ESPECIALLY LIGHT, DURABLE AND AESTHETIC CRANK DRIVE BY CAMPAGNOLO ARE PRESENTED IN THESE PHOTOGRAPHS FOR AN ARTICLE ÖN BICYCLES IN *SPORTS* MAGAZINE. (GER)

● **153** (ERSTE SEITE) «HOT BERTAA» – DER VON PHILIPPE STARCK ENTWORFENE WASSERKESSEL, AUFGENOMMEN FÜR ALESSI. (ITA)

● **154, 155** EINE HIGH-TECH-GANGSCHALTUNG DER NEUEN GENERATION UND EINE BESONDERS LEICHTE, STABILE UND ÄSTHETISCHE KURBELGARNITUR VON CAMPAGNOLO, FÜR EINEN ARTIKEL ÜBER FAHRRÄDER IN DER ZEITSCHRIFT*SPORTS*. (GER)

▲ **153** (PREMIÈRE PAGE) «HOT BERTAA», LA BOUILLOIRE CRÉÉE PAR PHILIPPE STARCK, PHOTOGRAPHIÉE POUR UNE BROCHURE. (ITA)

▲ **154, 155** LE DÉRAILLEUR D'UNE BICYCLETTE AVEC MULTIPLES CHANGEMENTS DE VITESSE ET L'AXE COUDÉ DE LA BICYCLETTE CAMPAGNOLO, PHOTOGRAPHIÉS POUR UN ARTICLE SUR LES BICYCLETTES, PARU DANS LE MAGAZINE *SPORTS*. (GER)

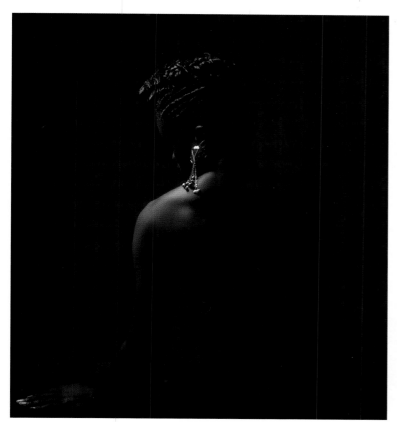

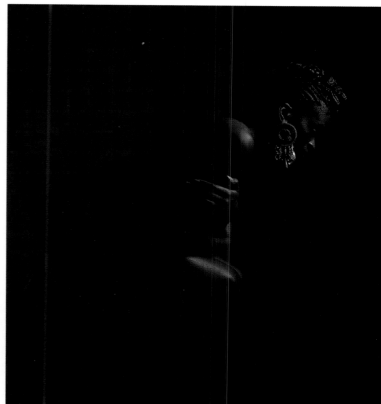

PHOTOGRAPHER:
HARRY WADE
CAMERA:
HASSELBLAD 2000
FCW, NIKON F4
FILM:
AGFAPAN 100
CLIENT:
CHERYL MOODY
JEWELRY DESIGN
ART DIRECTOR:
HARRY WADE
DESIGNER:
CHERYL MOODY
156-158

■ 156-158 A SIMPLE LIGHTING SET-UP WITH REFLECTORS WAS USED TO BRING OUT THE BODY HIGHLIGHTS IN THIS PHOTOGRAPH WHICH BELONGS TO AN AD CAMPAIGN FOR CHERYL MOODY'S JEWELRY. THE PHOTOG-RAPHER HAS BEEN WORKING ON LIGHTING AND SKIN COLOR FOR SEVERAL YEARS. (USA)

● 156-158 EINE EINFACHE BELEUCHTUNG MIT REFLEKTOREN WURDE FÜR DIESE AUFNAHME VERWENDET, DIE ZU EINER WERBEKAMPAGNE FÜR SCHMUCK VON CHERYL MOODY GEHÖRT. DER PHOTOGRAPH BEFASST SICH SEIT JAH-REN MIT DEM ZUSAMMENSPIEL VON BELEUCH-TUNG UND HAUT. (USA)

▲ 156-158 CETTE PHOTOGRAPHIE TIRÉE D'UNE CAMPAGNE DE PUBLICITÉ POUR LES BIJOUX DE CHERYL MOODY A ÉTÉ RÉALISÉE À L'AIDE D'UN ÉCLAIRAGE SIMPLE AVEC RÉ-FLECTEURS. LE PHOTOGRAPHE ÉTUDIE DE-PUIS DES ANNÉES LES JEUX DE LUMIÈRE SUR LA PEAU. (USA)

PHOTOGRAPHER:	CAMERA:	ART DIRECTOR:
IAN MCKINNELL	SINAR P2 4X5	MIKE TAYLOR
REPRESENTATIVE:	FILM:	AGENCY:
SPECIAL	FUJI VELVIA	UFFINDELL
PHOTOGRAPHERS	CLIENT:	& WEST
COMPANY	SIEBE PLC	159

■ 159 COMPRESSED AIR EQUIPMENT PHOTO-GRAPHED FOR A BROCHURE OF A MULTINA-TIONAL ENGINEERING COMPANY. THE PHOTO-GRAPH WAS TO BE GRAPHICALLY ILLUSTRA-TIVE RATHER THAN INFORMATIVE. (GBR)

■ 160-162 PRODUCTS FROM BANG & OLUFSEN PRESENTED AGAINST DANISH SCENERY RE-FERRING TO DANISH WRITERS AND ARTISTS SUCH AS HANS-CHRISTIAN ANDERSEN, KAREN BLIXEN, ETC. THE PHOTOGRAPHS WERE USED IN A B&O CONCEPT/IMAGE BROCHURE. (DEN)

● 159 PRESSLUFTAUSRÜSTUNG, PHOTOGRA-PHIERT FÜR DIE FIRMENBROSCHÜRE EINER MULTINATIONALEN MASCHINENBAUFIRMA. DIE AUFNAHME SOLLTE EHER GRAPHISCH UND ILLUSTRATIV ALS INFORMATIV SEIN. (GBR)

● 160-162 PRODUKTE VON BANG & OLUFSEN IN DÄNISCHER LANDSCHAFT AUFGENOMMEN, DIE EINEN BEZUG ZU DÄNISCHEN SCHRIFT-STELLERN UND KÜNSTLERN HAT, WIE ZUM BEISPIEL HANS-CHRISTIAN ANDERSEN UND KAREN BLIXEN. (DEN)

▲ 159 MATÉRIEL À AIR COMPRIMÉ PHOTOGRA-PHIÉ POUR LA BROCHURE D'UNE ENTREPRISE DE CONSTRUCTION DE MACHINES. L'EFFET VISUEL, GRAPHIQUE DE LA PHOTO IMPORTAIT PLUS QUE L'ASPECT INFORMATIF. (GBR)

▲ 160-162 DES PRODUITS DE BANG & OLUF-SEN PHOTOGRAPHIÉS DANS DES PAYSAGES DU DANEMARK QUI SONT ASSOCIÉS À DES ÉCRIVAINS ET DES ARTISTES DE CE PAYS, PAR EXEMPLE HANS-CHRISTIAN ANDERSEN ET KAREN BLIXEN. (DEN)

PHOTOGRAPHER:
POUL IB HENRIKSEN
CAMERA:
SINAR
FILM:
KODAK 6105
CLIENT:
BANG & OLUFSEN A/S

ART DIRECTOR:
MARIANNE BJARLOV
DESIGNER:
MARIANNE BJARLOV
AGENCY:
TED BATES
160-162

PHOTOGRAPHER:

J.P. SOTTO MAYOR

CAMERA:

LINHOF

FILM:

FUJI RDP 9X12

CLIENT:

SILAMPOS

ART DIRECTOR:

GIL MAIA

DESIGNER:

GIL MAIA

163, 164

■ **163, 164** THE PHOTOGRAPHER MADE USE OF THE REFLECTIVE PROPERTIES OF THE MATERIAL, USING GREEN AS A BACKGROUND IN ONE SHOT. THE GOLDEN HANDLES WERE TO BE THE CENTRAL MOTIF IN BOTH PHOTOGRAPHS USED IN A CATALOG. (POR)

● **190, 191** DER PHOTOGRAPH MACHTE SICH DIE REFLEXION DES MATERIALS ZUNUTZE. IN DER AUFNAHME DER BEIDEN TÖPFE GING ES VOR'ALLEM UM BETONUNG DER GOLDENEN HENKEL. DIE PHOTOS WURDEN IM KATALOG DES HERSTELLERS VERWENDET. (POR)

▲ **190, 191** LES FORMES DE L'AUTOCUISEUR ET DE LA CASSEROLE SONT MISES EN VALEUR PAR UN EFFET DE CLAIR-OBSCUR ET DE REFLETS. LES ÉLÉMENTS DORÉS CONSTITUENT LE MOTIF CENTRAL. D'UNE BROCHURE PUBLICITAIRE DU FABRICANT. (POR)

PHOTOGRAPHER: ART DIRECTOR:

RICK RUSING   KURT RIGGERT

CAMERA: DESIGNER:

SINAR 8X10   BILL TONNESON

FILM: AGENCY:

FUJI 50 DAYLIGHT   SCHOLZ & FRIENDS

CLIENT: 165-167

BMW AG

■ 165-167 PHOTOGRAPHS FROM A SERIES FOR THE BMW CORPORATE CALENDAR INTENDED FOR WORLD-WIDE DISTRIBUTION. THE CARS WERE SHOT ON LOCATION IN DEL TIBRE, SPAIN, WITH BACKGROUNDS DESIGNED BY AN ARCHITECT IN THE USA AND CONSTRUCTED IN SPAIN. (GER)

● 165-167 AUFNAHMEN AUS EINER SERIE FÜR DEN BMW-FIRMENKALENDER, DER WELTWEIT VERSANDT WIRD. DIE BMWS WURDEN IN DEL TIBRE, SPANIEN, AUFGENOMMEN, UND ZWAR VOR HINTERGRÜNDEN, DIE VON EINEM AMERI-KANISCHEN ARCHITEKTEN ENTWORFEN UND IN SPANIEN GEBAUT WURDEN. (GER)

▲ 165-167 PHOTOS D'UNE SÉRIE ILLUSTRANT LE CALENDRIER D'ENTREPRISE DE BMW, QUI EST DISTRIBUÉ DANS LE MONDE ENTIER. LES VOÎTURES ONT ÉTÉ PHOTOGRAPHIÉES À DEL TIBRE, EN ESPAGNE, DEVANT DES DÉCORS CRÉÉS PAR UN ARCHITECTE AMÉRICAIN ET CONSTRUITS SUR PLACE. (GER)

PHOTOGRAPHER:
BRUCE WOLF
REPRESENTATIVE:
STOCKLAND/MARTEL
CLIENT:
MARTEX/WEST POINT
PEPPERELL
ART DIRECTOR:
JAMES SEBASTIAN
DESIGNERS:
JUNKO MAYUMI,
JAMES SEBASTIAN
INTERIOR DESIGNER:
WILLIAM WALTER
AGENCY:
DESIGNFRAME INC.
168

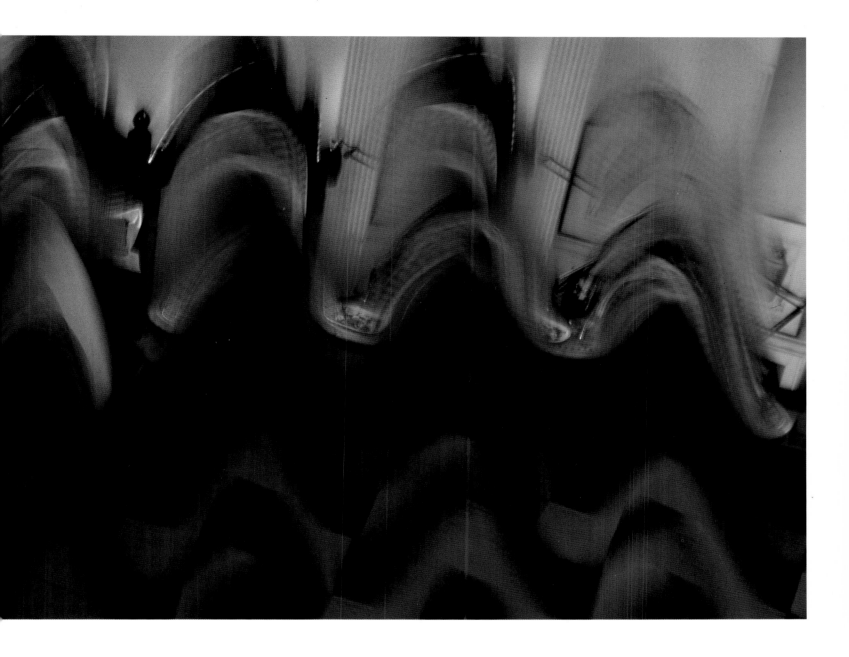

■ 168 THE PRIMARY INTENT OF THIS PHOTO-GRAPH WAS TO INTRODUCE THE NEW MARTEX PRODUCT LINE AND TO EMPHASIZE ITS CREA-TIVE IMAGE. THE IDEA WAS TO HEIGHTEN THE EXPERIENCE OF INTERIORS THROUGH MOTION WHILE ALSO FOCUSING ATTENTION ON THE PRODUCT. A SLIT-SCAN CAMERA, MOTION PICTURE LIGHTING EQUIPMENT AND STILL PHOTO TECHNIQUES WERE USED. (USA)

● 168 ES GING IN ERSTER LINIE UM DIE EIN-FÜHRUNG EINES NEUEN PRODUKTS DES HEIM-TEXTILIENHERSTELLERS MARTEX. UM DIE TEXTILIEN ZUM ERLEBNIS WERDEN ZU LASSEN UND DIE AUFMERKSAMKEIT AUF SIE ZU LENKEN, WURDE BEWEGUNG EINGESETZ. ES WURDE EINE SLIT-SCAN-KAMERA MIT EINER FILMBELEUCHTUNGSAUSRÜSTUNG SOWIE EINE STANDBILDTECHNIK VERWENDET. (USA)

▲ 168 L'OBJECTIF PREMIER ÉTAIT DE PRÉ-SENTER UN NOUVEAU PRODUIT DU FABRICANT MARTEX. LE MOUVEMENT A ÉTÉ UTILISÉ POUR DONNER VIE À UN INTÉRIEUR; CELA PERMET-TAIT EN MÊME TEMPS D'ATTIRER L'ATTENTION SUR LE LIT ET LE PRODUIT. LE PHOTOGRAPHE A UTILISÉ UN ÉQUIPEMENT DE TRAVELLING AVEC DES PROJECTEURS DE CINÉMA ET UNE INSTALLATION FIXE. (USA)

PHOTOGRAPHER:
TODD MERRITT HAIMAN
CAMERA:
NIKON F3
FILM:
FUJI VELVIA
CLIENT:
PUSH COMMUNICATIONS
169

BEST PRODUCT
PHOTOGRAPHER:
MICHAEL NORTHRUP
REPRESENTATIVE:
MARK THOMPSON
CAMERA:
BRONICA ETR
FILM:
VERICOLOR III
CLIENT:
THE GALLERY OF
MARKET EAST MALL

ART DIRECTORS:
TIM THOMPSON
DAVE PLUNKERT
DESIGNER:
DAVE PLUNKERT
STYLIST:
DAVE PLUNKERT
AGENCY:
GRAFFITO
> 170

■ 169 IN ORDER TO DRAW ATTENTION TO THIS TIRE'S ALL-TERRAIN CHARACTERISTICS, IT WAS PLACED WITHIN A ROUGH ENVIRONMENTAL SETTING (PAINTED DESERT NATIONAL PARK, ARIZONA) AND PHOTOGRAPHED AT DAWN TO CAPTURE THE UNIQUE AND COLORFUL LIGHT OF A DESERT SUNRISE. (USA)

■ 170 THIS PHOTOGRAPH FOR "THE GALLERY AT MARKET EAST MALL," IS USED ON A DIRECTORY BOARD FOR THE SHOPPING MALL. ALL SPECIAL EFFECTS WERE DONE IN FRONT OF THE CAMERA, INCLUDING STEAM, FRACTURING OF THE IMAGE (CREATED WITH A MASK) AND THE USE OF MULTIPLE FLASH EXPOSURES WITH COLORED GELS. (USA)

■ 169 UM DIE EIGNUNG DIESES REIFENS FÜR JEDES TERRAIN ZU UNTERSTREICHEN, WURDE IM PAINTED DESERT NATIONAL PARK IN ARIZONA PHOTOGRAPHIERT UND ZWAR IN DER MORGENDÄMMERUNG, UM DAS FARBENSPIEL UND DAS KLARE LICHT DES SONNENAUFGANGS IN DER WÜSTE EINZUFANGEN. (USA)

● 170 DIESE AUFNAHME FÜR DIE GALLERY AT MARKET EAST WURDE FÜR EINEN KATALOG VERWENDET. MEHRBFACHBELICHTUNG/BLITZ-LICHT MIT FARBFOLIEN AUF DEM BLITZ SORGTEN FÜR SPEZIELLE EFFEKTE, DIE ALLE VOR DER KAMERA ERFOLGTEN, EINSCHLIESSLICH DES DAMPFES UND DER MIT HILFE EINER MASKE ERREICHTEN «FRAKTUR». (USA)

▲ 169 CES PHOTOS ONT ÉTÉ RÉALISÉES DANS UN DÉSERT DE L'ARIZONA (PAINTED DESERT NATIONAL PARK) AFIN DE SOULIGNER LES QUALITÉS D'UN PNEU TOUT TERRAIN. LE PHOTOGRAPHE A TIRÉ PARTI DU JEU DES COULEURS ET DE LA LUMIÈRE LIMPIDE DU LEVER DU SOLEIL. (USA)

▲ 170 PHOTO RÉALISÉE POUR LE CATALOGUE DE LA GALLERY AT MARKET EAST. À L'AIDE D'ÉCLAIRAGES MULTIPLES ET DE LUMIÈRE DE FLASH AVEC GEL COLORÉ, DES EFFETS SPÉCIAUX ONT ÉTÉ OBTENUS AU MOMENT MÊME DE LA PHOTO, Y COMPRIS LA VAPEUR ET LA «FRACTURE», RÉALISÉE À L'AIDE D'UN MASQUE. (USA)

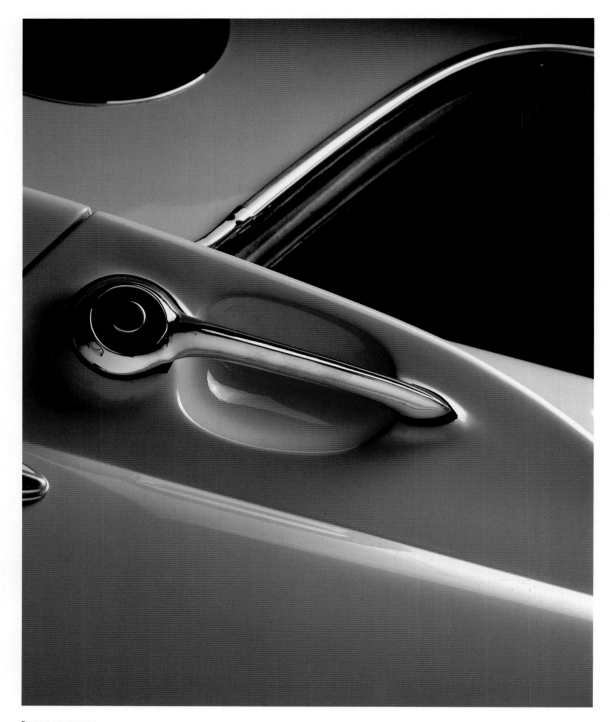

PHOTOGRAPHER:
DAVID PLANK
CLIENTS:
ARROWSMITH TYPE,
DONALD BLYLER OFF-
SET, FIDELITY COLOR,
DAVE LOOSE DESIGN,
DAVE PLANK
PHOTOGRAPHY
ART DIRECTOR:
DAVID LOOSE
DESIGNER:
LYNN RITTS
AGENCY:
DAVE LOOSE DESIGN
171, 172

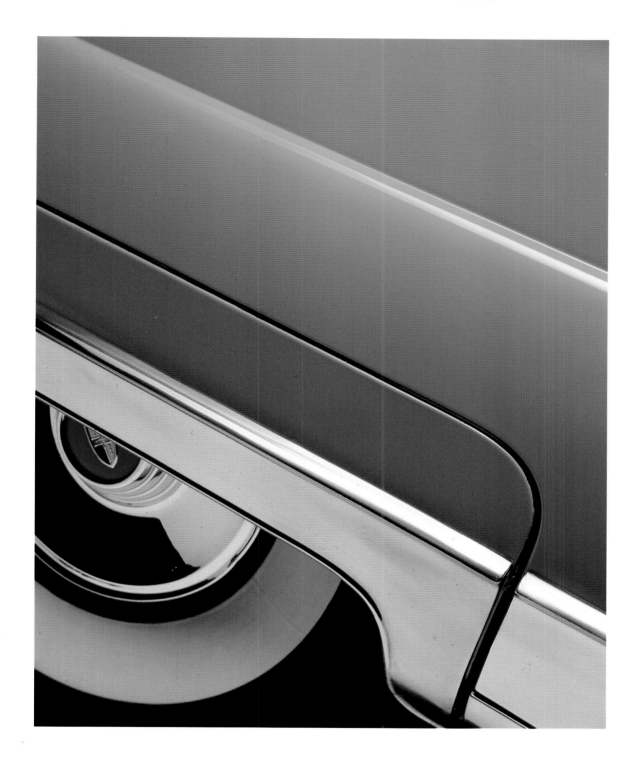

■ 171, 172 A LINCOLN COUPE CAPRI AND A 1957 T-BIRD WHICH, FOR REASONS OF WEATHER, TIME AND BUDGET, WERE PHOTOGRAPHED IN THE STUDIO. IN THIS CLASSIC CAR SERIES, THE PHOTOGRAPHER CHOSE TO HIGHLIGHT THOSE FEATURES FOR WHICH EACH CAR IS REMEMBERED. THE CARS WERE TRUCKED IN ON FLATBED TRAILERS AND ONLY FOUR HOURS WERE ALLOWED FOR EACH SHOOTING AS THE OWNERS WOULD NOT LEAVE THE CARS. (USA)

● 171, 172 EIN 1956ER LINCOLN COUPÉ CAPRI UND EIN 1957ER T-BIRD, AUS WETTER-, ZEIT- UND KOSTENGRÜNDEN IM STUDIO AUFGENOMMEN. SIE GEHÖREN ZU EINER KLASSIKER- REIHE, FÜR DIE DAVID PLANK DIE TYPISCHEN DETAILS PHOTOGRAPHIERTE. SIE WURDEN MIT EINEM TIEFLADER INS STUDIO GEBRACHT. DEM PHOTOGRAPHEN BLIEBEN VIER STUNDEN FÜR JEDES AUTO, DEREN BESITZER SIE NICHT AUS DEN AUGEN LASSEN WOLLTEN. (USA)

▲ 171, 172 PHOTOS D'UN COUPÉ LINCOLN CAPRI DE 1956 ET DE LA T-BIRD DE 1957 RÉA- LISÉES EN STUDIO. LE PHOTOGRAPHE A CHOI- SI DE REPRÉSENTER DES DÉTAILS CARAC- TÉRISTIQUES. CES VOITURES FURENT TRANS- PORTÉES SUR DES REMORQUES JUSQU'AU STUDIO; LE PHOTOGRAPHE NE DISPOSAIT QUE DE QUATRE HEURES POUR CHAQUE VOITURE, LES PROPRIÉTAIRES NE QUITTANT PAS CES MERVEILLES DES YEUX. (USA)

PHOTOGRAPHER:

JODY DOLE

CAMERA:

NIKON F4

CLIENT:

ESCADA

AGENCY:

WARING & LAROSA

173

PHOTOGRAPHER:

STEVE GERIG

CAMERA:

SINAR 4X5

FILM:

FUJI RDP 100

ART DIRECTOR:

STEVE GERIG

174

PHOTOGRAPHER:

NADAV KANDER

CLIENT:

LIBREX

ART DIRECTOR:

ERICH JOINER

AGENCY:

GOODBY BERLIN

SILVERSTEIN

175

■ 173 ONE OF AN UNPUBLISHED SERIES OF SIX EXPERIMENTAL PHOTOGRAPHS COMMISSIONED FOR AN AD CAMPAIGN FOR ESCADA PERFUME. THE PHOTOGRAPHER USED PRISMATIC LIGHTING GEAR DESIGNED AND BUILT BY HIMSELF. (USA)

■ 174 PHOTOGRAPH USED FOR SELF-PROMOTIONAL PURPOSES BY STEVE GEHRIG PHOTOGRAPHY, WICHITA. (USA)

■ 175 THIS PANORAMIC PHOTOGRAPH FOR AN AD CAMPAIGN FOR LIBREX NOTEBOOK COMPUTERS FOCUSES ON THE LANDSCAPE BY WAY OF EMPHASIZING THE KIND OF FREEDOM THE NOTEBOOK COMPUTER OFFERS. (USA)

● 173 AUS EINER SERIE EXPERIMENTELLER AUFNAHMEN, DIE FÜR EINE PARFUM-ANZEIGENKAMPAGNE IN AUFTRAG GEGEBEN WURDE. DER PHOTOGRAPH VERWENDETE EINE VON IHM ENTWORFENE UND GEBAUTE PRISMATISCHE BELEUCHTUNGSVORRICHTUNG. (USA)

● 174 ALS EIGENWERBUNG DES PHOTOGRAPHEN STEVE GEHRIG AUS WICHITA VERWENDETE AUFNAHME. (USA)

● 175 DIESE PANORAMA-AUFNAHME FÜR EINE KAMPAGNE FÜR LIBREX NOTEBOOK COMPUTER KONZENTRIERT SICH AUF DIE LANDSCHAFT, UM DIE DURCH DEN COMPUTER ERMÖGLICHTE MOBILITÄT DARZUSTELLEN. (USA)

▲ 173 D'UNE SÉRIE EXPÉRIMENTALE RÉALISÉE SUR COMMANDE POUR LA CAMPAGNE PUBLICITAIRE DU PARFUM ESCADA. LE PHOTOGRAPHE A UTILISÉ UNE INSTALLATION D'ÉCLAIRAGE PRISMATIQUE, QU'IL A CONÇUE ET CONSTRUITE LUI-MÊME. (USA)

▲ 174 CETTE PHOTO AUTOPROMOTIONNELLE A ÉTÉ RÉALISÉE AVEC UN APPAREIL SINAR 4X5 ET UNE PELLICULE FUJI RDP 100. (USA)

▲ 175 LE PAYSAGE CONSTITUE L'ÉLÉMENT DOMINANT DE CETTE PHOTO D'UNE CAMPAGNE POUR LIBREX NOTEBOOK COMPUTER: IL SYMBOLISE LA LIBERTÉ QUE CET ORDINATEUR PORTATIF OFFRE À SES UTILISATEURS. (USA)

PHOTOGRAPHER:

NADAV KANDER

CLIENT:

DUNHAM BOOTS

ART DIRECTOR:

JOHN DOYLE

AGENCY:

DOYLE ADVERTISING

& DESIGN, INC.

176, 177

■ 176, 177 THE DURABILITY AND HEAVY DUTY PROPERTIES OF DUNHAM BOOTS WERE TO BE EMPHASIZED IN THESE PHOTOGRAPHS SHOT ON LOCATION IN THE USA FOR AN ADVERTISING CAMPAIGN. (USA)

● 176, 177 DIE HALTBARKEIT UND ROBUSTHEIT VON DUNHAM-STIEFELN SOLLTE IN DIESEN AUFNAHMEN, DIE ON LOCATION IN DEN USA FÜR EINE WERBEKAMPAGNE ENTSTANDEN, ZUM AUSDRUCK KOMMEN. (USA)

▲ 176, 177 CES PHOTOS, RÉALISÉES POUR UNE CAMPAGNE DE PUBLICITÉ, DEVAIENT EXPRIMER LES QUALITÉS DE ROBUSTESSE ET LA SOLIDITÉ DES BOTTES DUNHAM. ELLES ONT ÉTÉ PRISES IN SITU AUX USA. (USA)

PHOTOGRAPHER:

ERNST HERMANN RUTH

CAMERA:

SINAR 4X5

FILM:

EKTACHROME 100 S

CLIENT:

EUROPE STUDIOS

ART DIRECTOR:

ERNST HERMANN RUTH

DESIGNER:

ERNST HERMANN RUTH

178, 179

■ **178, 179** THESE PHOTOGRAPHS OF DETAILS OF A VINTAGE 1953 BUICK SPECIAL COUPÉ WERE SHOT WITH ARTIFICIAL LIGHT, VARIOUS FILTERS FOR COLOR EFFECTS AND A SUPER WIDE-ANGLE LENS. USED AS SELF-PROMOTION BY EUROPE STUDIOS. (FRA)

● **178, 179** DETAILS EINES BUICK SPECIAL COUPÉ BAUJAHR 1953. DIE AUFNAHMEN, DIE ALS EIGENWERBUNG DER EUROPE STUDIOS DIENEN, WURDEN MIT KUNSTLICHT, EINEM SUPERWEITWINKELOBJEKTIV UND DIVERSEN FILTERN FÜR FARBEFFEKTE GEMACHT. (FRA)

▲ **178, 179** DÉTAILS D'UN COUPÉ BUICK SPÉ-CIAL DE 1953. PHOTOS, UTILISÉES COMME AUTOPROMOTION DES STUDIOS EUROPE ET RÉALISÉES À L'AIDE DE LUMIÈRE ARTIFI-CIELLE, D'UN OBJECTIF GRAND ANGLE ET DE FILTRES POUR LES COULEURS. (FRA)

PHOTOGRAPHER:
RJ MUNA
CLIENT:
ACUSON
ART DIRECTOR:
KEVIN ARCHER
AGENCY:
EVANS ADVERTISING
180, 181

■ 180, 181 DETAILS OF ACUSON COMPUTERS USED IN AN ADVERTISING CAMPAIGN. (USA)

■ 182, 183 THE PHOTOGRAPHER WAS ASSIGNED TO DO DIFFERING INTERPRETATIONS FOR THE ZETBE COLLECTION OF BRIEFCASES AND BAGS. THE PHOTOGRAPHS WERE THEN PRINTED AS POSTCARDS AND USED IN A PROMOTIONAL FOLDER. THESE TWO PHOTOGRAPHS WERE SHOT IN THE STUDIO, 182 WITH STRONG SUNLIGHT, 183 WITH FLASH. (GER)

● 180, 181 DETAILS VON ACUSON COMPU-TERN, FÜR EINE WERBEKAMPAGNE. (USA)

● 182, 183 MAPPEN UND TASCHEN AUS DER ZETBE-KOLLEKTION SOLLTEN UNTERSCHIED-LICH INTERPRETIERT WERDEN. SIE WERDEN ALS «ANSICHTSKARTEN» IN EINER PRÄSENTA-TIONSMAPPE VERWENDET. BEIDE AUFNAHMEN ENTSTANDEN IM STUDIO; FÜR 182 WURDE STARKES SONNENLICHT GENUTZT, 183 WURDE MIT BLITZLICHT PHOTOGRAPHIERT. (GER)

▲ 180, 181 DÉTAILS DES ORDINATEURS ACU-SON, POUR UNE CAMPAGNE DE PUB. (USA)

▲ 182, 183 INTERPRÉTATION PHOTOGRAPHI-QUE DES DIVERS CLASSEURS ET SACS DE LA COLLECTION ZETBE. PHOTOS UTILISÉES COMME «CARTES POSTALES» DANS UN CARTABLE DE PRÉSENTATION. LES DEUX PHO-TOS ONT ÉTÉ RÉALISÉES EN STUDIO, LA PREMIÈRE À LA LUMIÈRE DU SOLEIL, LA DEUXIÈME AVEC UN FLASH. (GER)

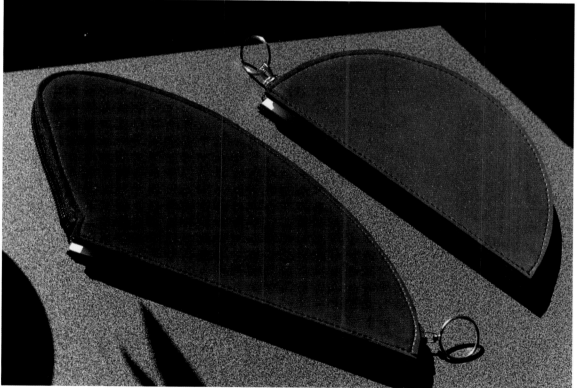

PHOTOGRAPHER:
EMANUEL RAAB
CAMERA:
CANON T90, ZENTA
BRONICA ETRS
CLIENT:
ZETBE

ART DIRECTOR:
EMANUEL RAAB
DESIGNERS:
MYRIAM GAUTSCHI,
GÜNTER ZÖLLER
AGENCY:
P.A.K.

182, 183

PHOTOGRAPHER:
GEORGE KAMPER
REPRESENTATIVE:
URSULA, INC.
CLIENT:
EASTMAN KODAK
COMPANY
ART DIRECTOR:
CRAIG BROWN
AGENCY:
SIGNIFICS, INC.
< 184

PHOTOGRAPHER:
HUNTER FREEMAN
REPRESENTATIVE:
BOBBI WENDT
CAMERA:
SINAR
FILM:
KODAK PROFESSIONAL
EKTACHROME
CLIENTS:
HUNTER FREEMAN
STUDIO, WOODS
LITHOGRAPHICS
ART DIRECTORS:
HUNTER FREEMAN,
BOBBI WENDT
DESIGNER:
KEN COOK
185

■ 184 PHOTOGRAPH FOR AN INTERNATIONAL AD CAMPAIGN BY EASTMAN KODAK. IT WAS SHOT IN 4X5 KODAK HC NEGATIVE MATERIAL. A 10X40 FOOT BANK WITH STROBES MIXED WITH HOT LIGHTS FOR STREAKS AND WARM COLOR WAS USED. (USA)

■ 185 "PEN ON PERFORATED METAL." THIS PHOTOGRAPH SERVES AS PROMOTION FOR THE PHOTOGRAPHER AND FOR THE SEPARATION AND PRINTING CAPABILITES (ON ULTRA-DOT 600 PRINTING SYSTEM) OF A LITHOGRAPHER/PRINTER. (USA)

● 184 AUFNAHME FÜR EINE INTERNATIONALE WERBEKAMPAGNE VON EASTMAN KODAK. DIE BELEUCHTUNG WAR EINE MISCHUNG VON STROBOSKOP- UND WARMEM LICHT, DIE DAZU DIENTE, DIE STREIFEN UND WARMEN TÖNE ZU BEKOMMEN. (USA)

● 185 «FÜLLFEDERHALTER AUF PERFORIERTEM METALL» – DIESE AUFNAHME DIENT ALS EIGENWERBUNG FÜR DEN PHOTOGRAPHEN UND FÜR DIE LITHO- UND DRUCKQUALITÄT (MIT ULTRADOT 600) EINER LITHOGRAPHENANSTALT/ DRUCKEREI. (USA)

▲ 184 PHOTO RÉALISÉE POUR UNE CAMPAGNE INTERNATIONALE D'EASTMAN KODAK. L'ÉCLAIRAGE SE COMPOSAIT D'UN MÉLANGE DE LUMIÈRE STROBOSCOPIQUE ET DE LUMIÈRE CHAUDE, AFIN D'OBTENIR DES BANDES ET DES TEINTES CHALEUREUSES. (USA)

▲ 185 «STYLO SUR MÉTAL PERFORÉ». PHOTO RÉALISÉE POUR WOODS LITHOGRAPHICS, ILLUSTRANT LA QUALITÉ DU SYSTÈME ULTRADOT 600, UTILISÉ PAR CETTE IMPRIMERIE. ELLE SERT ÉGALEMENT DE PUBLICITÉ À UN STUDIO DE PHOTOGRAPHIE. (USA)

PHOTOGRAPHER:
PATRICK ROHNER
CLIENT:
SWATCH
ART DIRECTOR:
LUIGI DEL MEDICO
AGENCY:
FARNER PUBLICIS
186-188

■ 186-188 FROM A SERIES OF 27 PHOTO-GRAPHS PRESENTING SWATCHES. THE AS-SIGNMENT WAS TO ESTABLISH A CORRELA-TION TO THE VARIOUS NAMES AND TYPES: "DA VINCI" (THIS NAME WAS LATER CHANGED), A DIVER'S WATCH AND "HIBISCUS." (SWI)

● 186-188 BEISPIELE AUS EINER REIHE VON INSGESAMT 27 AUFNAHMEN. DIE AUFGABE BE-STAND DARIN, EINEN BEZUG ZU DER JEWEI-LIGEN UHR ZU SCHAFFEN: «DA VINCI» (DIE-SER NAME WURDE SPÄTER GEÄNDERT), EINE TAUCHERUHR UND «HIBISKUS». (SWI)

▲ 186-188 EXEMPLES D'UNE SÉRIE DE 27 PHOTOGRAPHIES. IL S'AGISSAIT DE CRÉER UN RAPPORT ENTRE LES DIVERS TYPES DE MONTRES: «DA VINCI» (CE NOM A ÉTÉ CHANGÉ ULTÉRIEUREMENT), UNE MONTRE DE PLONGÉE ET «HIBISKUS». (SWI)

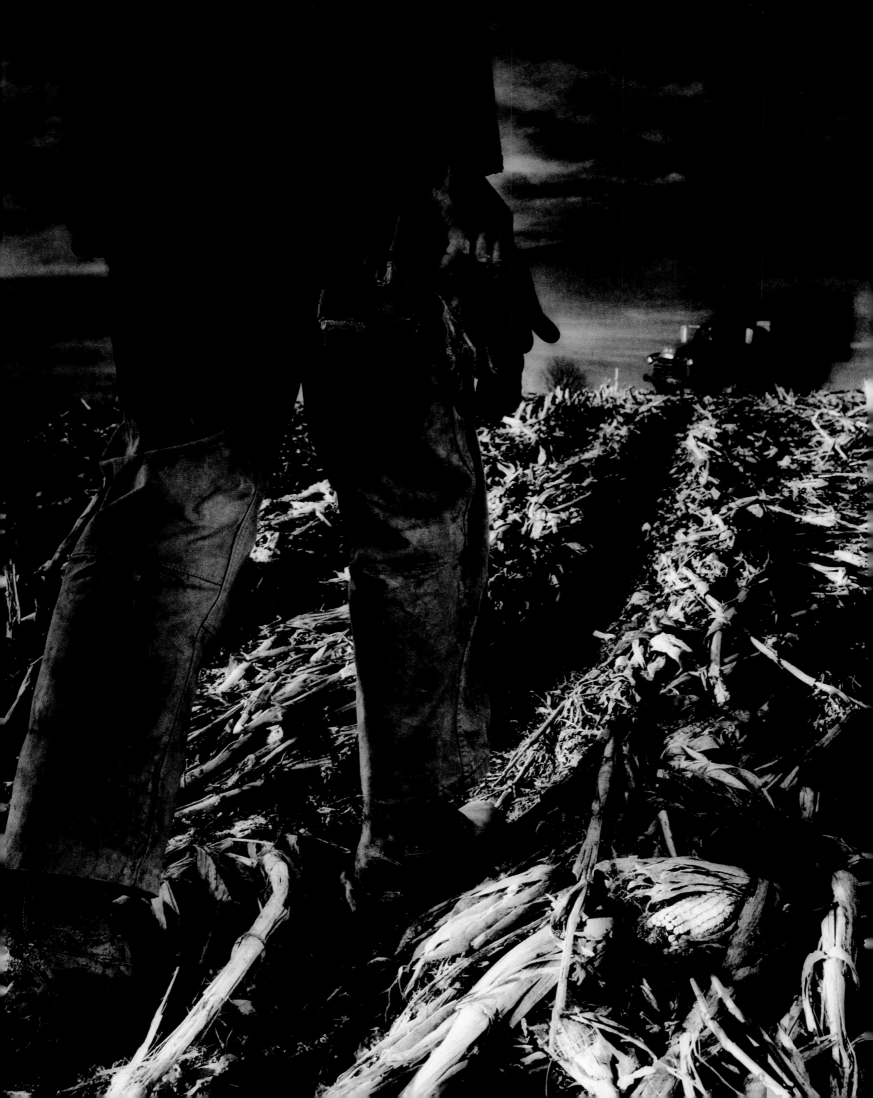

OUTDOOR

AUSSENAUFNAHMEN

EXTERIEURS

(FIRST PAGE OF
OUTDOOR SECTION)
Photographer:
NADAV KANDER
Client:
DUNHAM BOOTS
Art Director:
JOHN DOYLE
Designer:
JOHN DOYLE
Agency:
DOYLE ADVERTISING
& DESIGN, INC.
< 189

(THIS SPREAD)
PHOTOGRAPHER:
GUY KLOPPENBURG
ART DIRECTOR:
GUY KLOPPENBURG
DESIGNER:
GUY KLOPPENBURG
190, 191

■ 189 (FIRST PAGE OF OUTDOOR SECTION) A CORNFIELD AFTER THE HARVEST, PHOTO-GRAPHED IN THE USA FOR AN AD CAMPAIGN IN WHICH THE DURABILITY OF DUNHAM BOOTS HAD TO BE COMMUNICATED. (USA)

■ 190, 191 "'39 FORD, BEAUFORT COUNTY, NORTH CAROLINA" AND "BOWDEN'S CABIN, HYDE COUNTY, NORTH CAROLINA"—TWO SELF-PROMOTIONAL PHOTOGRAPHS. (USA)

● 189 (ERSTE SEITE) EIN ABGEERNTETES MAISFELD IN DEN USA, PHOTOGRAPHIERT FÜR EINE WERBEKAMPGNE FÜR DUNHAM-STIEFEL, DEREN STRAPAZIERFÄHIGKEIT DEMONSTRIERT WERDEN SOLLTE. (USA)

● 190, 191 "'39 FORD, BEAUFORT COUNTY, NORTH CAROLINA" UND "BOWDEN'S CABIN, HYDE COUNTY, NORTH CAROLINA" – ALS EIGEN-WERBUNG VERWENDETE AUFNAHMEN. (USA)

▲ 189 (PREMIÈRE PAGE) UN CHAMP DE MAÏS FRAÎCHEMENT RÉCOLTÉ AUX ÉTATS-UNIS, PHOTOGRAPHIÉ POUR UNE CAMPAGNE DE PUBLICITÉ POUR LES BOTTES DUNHAM, ILLUS-TRANT LEUR DURABILITÉ. (USA)

▲ 190, 191 "'39 FORD, BEAUFORT COUNTY, NORTH CAROLINA" ET "BOWDEN'S CABIN, HYDE COUNTY, NORTH CAROLINA". DEUX PHOTOS UTILISÉES COMME AUTOPROMOTION. (USA)

(TOP)

PHOTOGRAPHER:

TIM BIEBER

CAMERA:

FUJI 6X9

FILM:

FUJI RDP 100

DESIGNER:

STEVE LISKA

AGENCY:

LISKA

& ASSOCIATES

192

(BOTTOM)

PHOTOGRAPHER:

CONSTANTINE

MANOS

REPRESENTATIVE:

MAGNUM PHOTOS

CAMERA:

LEICA M-6

FILM:

KODACHROME 64

193

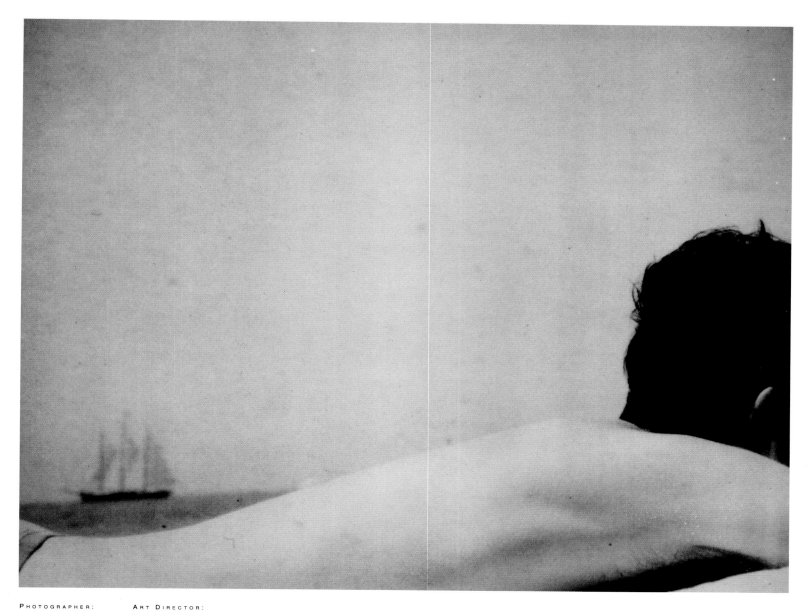

PHOTOGRAPHER:
BARBARA COLE
REPRESENTATIVE:
ANNE POWELL
CLIENTS:
BARBARA COLE
PHOTOGRAPHY;
ESKIND WADDELL,
GRAPHIC SPECIAL-
TIES; MACKINNON-
MONCUR LTD.,
PROVINCIAL
PAPERS

ART DIRECTOR:
MALCOLM WADDELL
DESIGNERS:
SANDI KING,
GLENDA RISSMAN,
PETER SCOTT,
MALCOLM WADDELL
194

■ 192 PHOTOGRAPH FROM A SERIES USED FOR SELF-PROMOTION. (USA)

■ 193 HAMPTON BEACH, NEW HAMPSHIRE, A PHOTOGRAPH FROM A SERIES OF IMAGES THAT FORM A STRONG PERSONAL STATEMENT ABOUT THE UNITED STATES. (USA)

■ 194 "SHIP AT SEA"—EXAMPLE FROM A SERIES OF 13 IMAGES TAKEN IN THE SOUTH OF FRANCE AND ITALY ON POLAPAN AND POLAGRAPH INSTANT FILMS FOR A SELF-PRO-MOTIONAL CALENDAR. (CAN)

● 192 AUFNAHME AUS EINER REIHE, DIE ALS EIGENWERBUNG VERWENDET WURDE. (USA)

● 193 HAMPTON BEACH, NEW HAMPSHIRE – DIE SCHÖNHEIT DER LANDSCHAFT IN DEN USA WAR GEGENSTAND EINER FREIEN REIHE VON AUFNAHMEN DES PHOTOGRAPHEN. (USA)

● 194 «SHIP AT SEA» – AUS EINER REIHE VON AUFNAHMEN, DIE IM SÜDEN FRANKREICHS UND ITALIENS MIT POLAPAN UND POLAGRAPH INSTANT-FILMMATERIAL FÜR EINEN KALENDER GEMACHT WURDEN. (CAN)

▲ 192 PHOTO TIRÉE D'UNE SÉRIE QUI A ÉTÉ UTILISÉE COMME AUTOPROMOTION. (USA)

▲ 193 HAMPTON BEACH, NEW HAMPSHIRE. LA BEAUTÉ DU PAYSAGE AMÉRICAIN ÉTAIT LE SUJET DE CETTE SÉRIE D'ÉTUDES PERSON-NELLES DE CE PHOTOGRAPHE. (USA)

▲ 194 «BATEAU SUR LA MER». EXEMPLE D'UNE SÉRIE DE PHOTOS PRISES DANS LE SUD DE LA FRANCE ET EN ITALIE, SUR PELLICULES INS-TANTANÉES POLAPAN ET POLAGRAPH, POUR UN CALENDRIER AUTOPROMOTIONNEL. (CAN)

(TOP)

PHOTOGRAPHER:

HARRY DE ZITTER

CAMERA:

LINHOF MASTER TECH-

NIKA & TECHNIKARDAN

FILM:

FUJI VELVIA

CLIENT:

THE NEW ENGLAND LIFE

ART DIRECTOR:

TOM SIMONS

AGENCY:

PARTNERS AND SIMONS

195

(BOTTOM AND

OPPOSITE PAGE)

PHOTOGRAPHER:

HARRY DE ZITTER

CAMERA:

LINHOF MASTER TECH-

NIKA & TECHNIKARDAN

FILM:

FUJI VELVIA

PUBLISHER:

TEXAS MONTHLY

ART DIRECTOR:

D.J. STOUT

DESIGNER:

D.J. STOUT

> 196-198

■ **195** THE LOOK AND SPIRIT OF NEW ENGLAND, CAPTURED IN THIS PHOTOGRAPH FOR THE NEW ENGLAND LIFE COMPANY. IT IS PART OF AN ONGOING SERIES. (USA)

■ **196-198** "VANISHING TEXAS"—THESE PHOTOGRAPHS WERE ASSIGNED FOR AN EDITORIAL PHOTO ESSAY BY *TEXAS MONTHLY* MAGAZINE. (USA)

● **195** DIE SCHÖNHEIT UND DER GEIST DER LANDSCHAFT NEUENGLANDS, EINGEFANGEN IN EINER AUFNAHME FÜR EINE VERSICHERUNGSGESELLSCHAFT IN NEW ENGLAND. (USA)

● **196-198** DIESE AUFNAHMEN ENTSTANDEN FÜR EINEN PHOTO-ESSAY IN DER ZEITSCHRIFT *TEXAS MONTHLY* ÜBER DAS «VERSCHWINDENDE TEXAS». (USA)

▲ **195** CETTE PHOTO RÉALISÉE POUR UNE COMPAGNIE D'ASSURANCES DE LA NOUVELLE-ANGLETERRE, REFLÈTE BIEN LA BEAUTÉ DES PAYSAGES DE CET ÉTAT. (USA)

▲ **196-198** CES PHOTOS ONT ÉTÉ RÉALISÉES POUR UN REPORTAGE SUR LE «TEXAS QUI DISPARAIT», PUBLIÉ DANS LE MAGAZINE *TEXAS MONTHLY*. (USA)

PHOTOGRAPHER:
CHARLES WEBER
CAMERA:
MAMIYA 645
FILM:
EKTACHROME 100 PLUS
PUBLISHER:
EDITIONS OLIZANE
< 199, 200

PHOTOGRAPHER:
ROBERT MIZONO
CLIENT:
SQUAW CREEK RESORT
ART DIRECTOR:
MATT HALIGMAN
AGENCY:
ATLAS, CITRON, HALIG-
MAN & BEDECARRE
201

■ 199, 200 "THE SWISS GARDEN" (JARDIN SUISSE), A SERIES OF PHOTOGRAPHS COMMISSIONED BY THE MUSÉE DE L'ÉLYSÉE OF LAUSANNE FOR THE OCCASION OF SWITZERLAND'S 700TH ANNIVERSARY. IT WAS PUBLISHED IN A BOOK. (SWI)

■ 201 SUMMER ACTIVITIES IN WINTERTIME— PHOTOGRAPH FOR SQUAW CREEK HOLIDAY RESORT. (USA)

● 199, 200 «GARTEN SCHWEIZ» (JARDIN SUISSE), EINE IM AUFTRAG DES MUSÉE DE L'ÉLYSÉE ENTSTANDENE SERIE VON AUFNAHMEN ANLÄSSLICH DER 700-JAHR-FEIER DER SCHWEIZ. DIE PHOTOGRAPHIEN WURDEN IN BUCHFORM VERÖFFENTLICHT. (SWI)

● 201 SOMMERFREUDEN IM WINTER – EINE AUFNAHME FÜR DEN FERIENORT SQUAW CREEK IN DEN USA. (USA)

▲ 199, 200 «JARDIN SUISSE». PHOTOS TIRÉES D'UNE SÉRIE RÉALISÉE SUR MANDAT DU MUSÉE DE L'ÉLYSÉE DE LAUSANNE, À L'OCCASION DU 700E ANNIVERSAIRE DE LA CONFÉDÉRATION HELVÉTIQUE, ET PUBLIÉE SOUS FORME DE LIVRE. (SWI)

▲ 201 DISTRACTIONS ESTIVALES EN HIVER. PHOTO POUR LE SQUAW CREEK, UN LIEU DE VILLÉGIATURE AUX ÉTATS-UNIS. (USA)

PHOTOGRAPHER:
ANDREAS
MÜLLER-POHLE
202

PHOTOGRAPHER:

CHRISTOPHER GREEN

CAMERA:

GOWLAND 4X5 POCKET

FILM:

KODAK 4, FUJI NSP

203, 204

■ **202** THIS IMAGE BELONGS TO A SERIES OF WORK UNDER THE THEME OF "VACANT CENTER." ITS PURPOSE IS TO DISTURB THE COMMON WAY OF LOOKING AT PHOTOGRAPHS: BY VACATING THE CENTER OF THE IMAGE AND PUSHING THINGS TO ITS BORDERS, THE PHOTOGRAPHER FORCES THE VIEWER'S EYE TO JUMP. THINGS ARE DISSOLVED INTO FACTS, DEFINITIONS INTO REALITIES. (GER)

■ **203, 204** A VISUAL STUDY OF SUMMER AND WINTER AT CRAIGVILLE BEACH ON CAPE COD, SHOT FOR THE MASSACHUSETTS ARTS LOTTERY COUNCIL. (USA))

● **202** AUS EINER GRUPPE VON ARBEITEN, DIE UNTER DEM STICHWORT «LEERE MITTE» ENTSTANDEN SIND. IHRE ABSICHT IST, DIE GEWOHNTE LESART VON PHOTOS ZU STÖREN: INDEM DER PHÓTOGRAPH DIE BILDMITTE ENTLEERTE UND DIE DINGE AN DEN RAND TREIBT, ZWINGT ER DAS AUGE ZU SPRINGEN. ER LÖST SACHEN IN SACHVERHALTE, DEFINITIONEN IN RELATIONEN AUF. (GER)

● **203, 204** EINE VISUELLE STUDIE VON SOMMER UND WINTER AN DER CRAIGVILLE BEACH VON CAPE COD, EINEM BELIEBTEN KÜSTENORT IN MASSACHUSETTS. (USA)

▲ **202** PHOTO TIRÉE D'UNE SÉRIE INTITULÉE «CENTRE VIDE»: LE PHOTOGRAPHE A CHOISI DE CONCENTRER LES MOTIFS SUR LES BORDS DE L'IMAGE, LE CENTRE RESTANT VIDE, AFIN DE TRANSFORMER LA PERCEPTION VISUELLE DU SPECTATEUR. L'ŒIL EST AINSI OBLIGÉ DE PASSER D'UN POINT À UN AUTRE; LES OBJETS DEVIENNENT DES FAITS, LES DÉFINITIONS DES RELATIONS. (GER)

▲ **203, 204** UNE INTERPRÉTATION VISUELLE DE L'ÉTÉ ET DE L'HIVER À CRAIGVILLE BEACH DE CAPE COD, UNE STATION BALNÉAIRE DU MASSACHUSETTS. (USA)

PHOTOGRAPHER:
PHILIP QUIRK
REPRESENTATIVE:
WILDLIGHT PHOTO
AGENCY
CAMERA:
LINHOF TECHNORAMA
FILM:
FUJICHROME 100, 6X17
CLIENT:
TOMASETTI PAPER
ART DIRECTOR:
MIMMO COZZOLINO
DESIGNER:
PHIL ELLETT
AGENCY:
COZZOLINO/ELLETT
DESIGN D'VISION
205

■ 205 PHOTOGRAPHER PHILIP QUIRK SAW THE STORM COMING FROM HIS STUDIO AT BONDI BEACH (AUSTRALIA). HE TOOK OÙT HIS CAMERA AND PHOTOGRAPHED THROUGH THE RAINLESS STORM. THE PHOTOGRAPH WAS USED IN A PROMOTIONAL POSTER FOR TOMASETTI PAPER. (AUS)

● 205 VON SEINEM STUDIO AN DER BONDI BEACH (STRAND IN AUSTRALIEN) AUS SAH DER PHOTOGRAPH DEN STURM KOMMEN, NAHM SEINE KAMERA UND PHOTOGRAPHIERTE DURCH DEN REGENLOSEN STURM. DIE AUFNAHME WURDE FÜR EIN PLAKAT FÜR TOMASETTI-PAPIER VERWENDET. (AUS)

▲ 205 LE PHOTOGRAPHE ÉTAIT DANS SON STUDIO DE BONDI BEACH (EN AUSTRALIE), LORSQU'IL VIT L'ORAGE ARRIVER; SAISISSANT SON APPAREIL, IL FIT DES PHOTOS DANS CETTE ATMOSPHÈRE ·D'ORAGE SANS PLUIE. CELLE-CI FUT REPRODUITE SUR UNE AFFICHE POUR LE PAPIER TOMASETTI. (AUS)

PHOTOGRAPHER:
STEPHEN WILKES
REPRESENTATIVE:
DOUG BROWN
CAMERA:
FUJICA GS 617
FILM:
FUJI 120
DESIGNER:
KURT JENNINGS
206, 207

PHOTOGRAPHER:
NADAV KANDER
CLIENT:
DUNHAM BOOTS
ART DIRECTOR:
JOHN DOYLE
DESIGNER:
JOHN DOYLE
AGENCY:
DOYLE ADVERTISING
& DESIGN, INC.
> 208

■ **206, 207** PHOTOGRAPHS FOR A SELF-PROMOTIONAL PIECE FOR THE PHOTOGRAPHER. THE FIRST WAS TAKEN AT WELLFLEET, MASSACHUSETTS, THE SECOND AT GLACIER NATIONAL PARK, MONTANA. (USA)

■ **208** FROM A SERIES PHOTOGRAPHED ON LOCATION IN THE USA FOR AN ADVERTISING CAMPAIGN FOR DUNHAM BOOTS. (USA)

● **206, 207** DIESE AUFNAHMEN ENTSTANDEN IN WELLFLEET, IM STAAT MASSACHUSETTS, UND IM GLACIER NATIONAL PARK, MONTANA, USA. SIE DIENTEN ALS EIGENWERBUNG DES PHOTOGRAPHEN. (USA)

● **208** AUS EINER REIHE VON AUFNAHMEN, DIE IN DEN USA FÜR EINE WERBEKAMPAGNE FÜR DUNHAM-STIEFEL GEMACHT WURDEN. (USA)

▲ **206, 207** PHOTOGRAPHIES SERVANT D'AUTOPROMOTION AU PHOTOGRAPHE. LA PREMIÈRE PHOTO A ÉTÉ PRISE À WELLFLEET, DANS LE MASSACHUSETTS, LA SECONDE AU GLACIER NATIONAL PARK DE MONTANA. (USA)

▲ **208** D'UNE SÉRIE DE PHOTOS QUI ONT ÉTÉ PRISES AUX USA, POUR UNE CAMPAGNE DE PUBLICITÉ DES BOTTES DUNHAM. (USA)

BEST OUTDOOR

PHOTOGRAPHER:

PETE STONE

REPRESENTATIVE:

BIG CITY

PRODUCTIONS

DESIGNER:

STEVEN SANDSTROM

AGENCY:

SANDSTROM

DESIGN, INC.

209

PHOTOGRAPHER:

ANGELICA M. ALVAREZ

210

■ **209** THIS PHOTOGRAPH WAS TAKEN AT BONDI BEACH, SYDNEY, IN A SALT WATER SWIMMING POOL. IT WAS USED AS SELF-PROMOTION. (AUS)

■ **210** FREE STUDY BY ANGELICA M. ALVAREZ, A STUDENT IN THE ART HISTORY DEGREE PROGRAM IN THE SCHOOL OF ART AT LOUISIANA STATE UNIVERSITY. (USA)

● **209** DIESE AUFNAHME ENTSTAND IN EINEM SALZWASSER-SWIMMING-POOL AN DER BONDI BEACH IN SYDNEY. SIE WURDE ALS EIGENWERBUNG VERWENDET. (AUS)

● **210** EINE FREIE STUDIE DER STUDENTIN ANGELICA M. ALVAREZ, DIE AN DER SCHOOL OF ART DER LOUISIANA STATE UNIVERSITY KUNSTGESCHICHTE STUDIERT. (USA)

▲ **209** CETTE PHOTO A ÉTÉ RÉALISÉE DANS UNE PISCINE D'EAU SALÉE DE BONDI BEACH À SIDNEY. ELLE A ÉTÉ UTILISÉE COMME AUTOPROMOTION. (AUS)

▲ **210** ÉTUDE PERSONNELLE RÉALISÉE PAR UNE ÉTUDIANTE EN HISTOIRE DE L'ART AUPRÈS DE LA LOUISIANA STATE UNIVERSITY, ANGELICA M. ALVAREZ. (USA)

PHOTOGRAPHER:
AERNOUT OVERBEEKE
REPRESENTATIVES:
ARTS COUNSEL (USA),
HILARY BRADFORD
(ITA), CHRISTA
KLUBERT (GER)
CAMERA:
LINHOF 6X17
FILM:
VERICOLOR III
ART DIRECTOR:
AERNOUT OVERBEEKE
211, 212

PHOTOGRAPHER:
ANDREAS PAUL
ELLMERER
CAMERA:
CONTAX RTS
FILM:
KODAK TRI-X
CLIENT:
FASHION PLATE
A.P. ELLMERER
DESIGNER:
BEN GRANZER
STYLIST:
ULRIEKE RIEFKE
213

■ 211 PHOTOGRAPH TAKEN DURING A LOCA-TION HUNT IN AUSTRALIA. THE ROCKS POINT-ING OUT OF THE WATER ARE CALLED "THE 12 APOSTLES" (POINT CAMPBELL). (NLD)

■ 212 A PORTRAIT OF A DOG TAKEN IN THE COUNTRYSIDE NEAR STRATFORD ST. MARY, ENGLAND. (NLD)

■ 213 AT THE HARBOR ENTRANCE TO CUX-HAVEN. WITH THE CHOICE OF THIS LOCATION IN GERMANY, THE PHOTOGRAPHER WANTED TO PROVE THAT THERE ARE GOOD LOCATIONS RIGHT IN FRONT OF ONE'S DOOR. (GER)

● 211 DIESE AUFNAHME ENTSTAND WÄHREND EINER LOCATION-SUCHE IN AUSTRALIEN. DIE AUS DEM WASSER RAGENDEN FELSEN WERDEN «DIE ZWÖLF APOSTEL» GENANNT. (NLD)

● 212 PORTRÄT EINES HUNDES, AUFGENOM-MEN AUF DEM LANDE IN DER NÄHE VON STRATFORD ST. MARY, ENGLAND. (NLD)

● 213 AN DER HAFENEINFAHRT VON CUXHA-VEN. MIT DER WAHL DIESER LOCATION WOLL-TE DER PHOTOGRAPH BEWEISEN, DASS SICH GUTE AUFNAHMEORTE AUCH VOR DER EIGE-NEN TÜR FINDEN LASSEN. (GER)

▲ 211 PHOTO RÉALISÉE EN AUSTRALIE, AU COURS DE LA RECHERCHE D'UN LIEU DE PRISES DE VUE. LES RÉCIFS SONT APPELÉS «LES 12 APÔTRES» (NLD)

▲ 212 PORTRÄT D'UN CHIEN PHOTOGRAPHIÉ À LA CAMPAGNE PRÈS DE STRATFORD ST. MARY EN ANGLETERRE. (NLD)

▲ 213 L'ENTRÉE DU PORT DE CUXHAVEN EN ALLEMAGNE. EN CHOISISSANT CET ENDROIT, LE PHOTOGRAPHE VOULAIT PROUVER QU'IL ÉTAIT POSSIBLE DE TROUVER DES BONS SUJETS TOUT PRÈS DE CHEZ SOI. (GER)

ARCHITECTURE

ARCHITEKTUR

ARCHITECTURE

(FIRST PAGE OF ARCHI-
TECTURE SECTION)
PHOTOGRAPHER:
BOB SHIMER
REPRESENTATIVE:
HEDRICH-BLESSING
CLIENT:
TRIZEC CORP.
ART DIRECTOR:
TIEM ONG-LEE
DESIGNER:
ONG-LEE DESIGN
< 214

PHOTOGRAPHER:
RAYMOND DEPARDON
REPRESENTATIVE:
KIM DOAN/MAGNUM
PHOTOS
CLIENT:
MAISON DES JEUNES ET
DE LA CULTURE
ART DIRECTOR:
CATHERINE GADON
DESIGNERS:
PASCAL CHALLIER,
LAURENCE FONTAINE
215

■ 214 (FIRST PAGE OF ARCHITECTURE SEC-
TION) PHOTOGRAPH PROMOTING AN OFFICE
BUILDING IN CALGARY, CANADA. SHOT AT
DAWN, A POLARIZER AND 81D FILTER WERE
USED TO ENHANCE THE COLORS OF THE EKTA-
CHROME FILM. A LONG LENS HELPED COM-
PRESS THE STRUCTURES. (CAN)

■ 215 PHOTOGRAPH FROM THE CATALOG FOR
AN EXHIBITION DEDICATED TO SCULPTORS
AND PHOTOGRAPHERS OF VALENCE, FRANCE.
THE THEME WAS THEIR COOPERATION WITH
LOCAL FIRMS. (FRA)

■ 216 A PERSONAL STUDY OF A BUILDING IN
DOWNTOWN SEATTLE. (USA)

● 214 (ERSTE SEITE) WERBUNG FÜR EIN
BÜROGEBÄUDE IN CALGARY. EIN POLARIZER
UND 81D FILTER WURDEN VERWENDET, UM
DAS LICHT UND DIE FARBEN DES EKTA-
CHROME-100-DAYLIGHT-FILMS ZU BEEINFLUS-
SEN. UM DIE STRUKTUREN ZU VERDICHTEN
WURDE EIN TELEOBJEKTIV BENUTZT. (CAN)

● 215 AUFNAHME AUS EINEM KATALOG FÜR
EINE AUSSTELLUNG, DIE BILDHAUERN UND
PHOTOGRAPHEN DER STADT VALENCE GEWID-
MET WAR. THEMA WAR IHRE ZUSAMMENARBEIT
MIT LOKALEN FIRMEN. (FRA)

● 216 PERSÖNLICHE STUDIE EINES GEBÄUDES
IM ZENTRUM VON SEATTLE. (USA)

▲ 214 (PREMIÈRE PAGE) PHOTO SERVANT DE
PUBLICITÉ À UN BUREAU DE CALGARY, CANA-
DA. ON A UTILISÉ UN POLARISEUR ET UN FIL-
TRE 81D POUR ACCENTUER LES COULEURS DE
LA PELLICULE EKTACHROME 100 LUMIÈRE
NATURELLE ET UN OBJECTIF GRAND ANGLE
POUR INTENSIFIER LES STRUCTURES. (CAN)

▲ 215 PHOTO TIRÉE DU CATALOGUE D'UNE
EXPOSITION ORGANISÉE À VALENCE ET CON-
SACRÉE À DES PLASTICIENS ET DES PHOTO-
GRAPHES AYANT TRAVAILLÉ AVEC DES ENTRE-
PRISES LOCALES. (FRA)

▲ 216 ÉTUDE PERSONNELLE D'UN BÂTIMENT
DANS LE CENTRE DE SEATTLE. (USA)

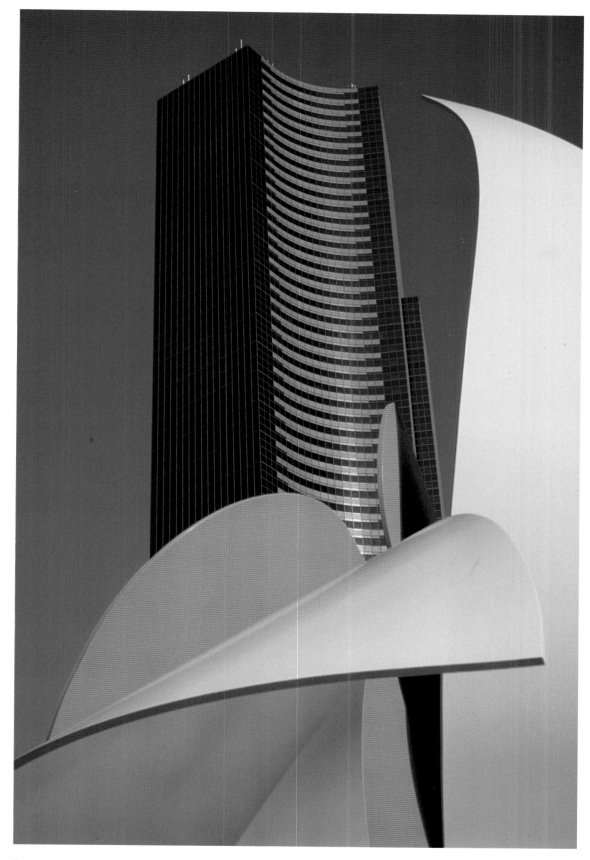

PHOTOGRAPHER:

JIANJUN SUN

CAMERA:

NIKON F4

FILM:

FUJICHROME VELVIA

216

PHOTOGRAPHER:
STEFAN KIESS

REPRESENTATIVE:
INGE METZGER

GMBH

CAMERA:
NIKON F2

FILM:
KODAK HIGH SPEED

INFRA RED

< 217

PHOTOGRAPHER:
RICHARD MANDELKORN

REPRESENTATIVE:
TOM GOODMAN

CAMERA:
SINAR P2 4X5

FILM:
FUJI RTP 4X5

CLIENT:
JUNG/BRANNEN

ASSOCIATES

218

■ 217 THE HENNINGER TOWER IN FRANKFURT AM MAIN. IN ORDER TO CONCENTRATE ON FORMAL ASPECTS AND TO OBTAIN A CERTAIN DEGREE OF ABSTRACTION, BLACK-AND-WHITE FILM WAS CHOSEN. (GER)

■ 218 THE ATRIUM MALL IN NEWTON HOUSING HIGH-END RETAILERS. THE ASSIGNMENT HAD BEEN TO REFLECT THE ELEGANCE OF THE INTERIOR DESIGN. (USA)

● 217 DER HENNINGER TURM IN FRANKFURT AM MAIN. UM EINE REDUKTION AUF DIE FORMALEN ASPEKTE UND EINE GEWISSE ABSTRAHIERUNG ZU ERREICHEN. WURDE SCHWARZWEISSFILMMATERIAL GEWÄHLT. (GER)

● 218 DIE ATRIUM-PASSAGE IN NEWTON, MASSACHUSETTS, MIT LÄDEN DER GEHOBENEN KLASSE. ES GALT, DIE ELEGANZ DER INNENARCHITEKTUR DARZUSTELLEN. (USA)

▲ 217 LA TOUR HENNINGER À FRANCFORT-SUR-LE-MAIN. LE PHOTOGRAPHE A ADOPTÉ LE NOIR ET BLANC, AFIN DE SE LIMITER AUX ASPECTS FORMELS ET PARVENIR À UN CERTAIN DEGRÉ D'ABSTRACTION. (GER)

▲ 218 LA GALERIE MARCHANDE THE ATRIUM MALL, À NEWTON. IL S'AGISSAIT DE REPRÉSENTER L'ÉLÉGANCE DE L'ARCHITECTURE INTÉRIEURE. (USA)

PHOTOGRAPHER:
JIM HEDRICH
REPRESENTATIVE:
HEDRICH-BLESSING
CLIENT:
MAGUIRE/THOMAS
PARTNERS
ART DIRECTOR:
LOWELL WILLIAMS
DESIGN
DESIGNER:
RICHARD LEGORETTO
219

PHOTOGRAPHER:
NICK MERRICK
REPRESENTATIVE:
HEDRICH-BLESSING
CLIENT:
HERMAN MILLER, INC.
ART DIRECTOR:
STEVE FRYKHOLM
ARCHITECT:
FRANK GEHRY & ASSOC.
220

PHOTOGRAPHER:
WAYNE CABLE
REPRESENTATIVE:
KIMBERLY GRIFFITHS
CAMERA:
HORSEMAN 4X5
FILM:
KODAK TECH PAN
CLIENT:
CHICAGO BOARD
OF TRADE
ART DIRECTOR:
DANA ARNETT
> 221

■ 219 PHOTOGRAPH OF AN OFFICE BUILDING RECEPTION FOYER AT SOLANA-IBM CENTER. IT WAS SHOT USING MOSTLY NATURAL LIGHT. THE FIGURE POSING IN THE DOORWAY WAS TO GIVE AN IDEA OF THE SCALE. (USA)

■ 220 DETAIL VIEW OF A FACTORY THAT PRODUCES HERMAN MILLER FURNITURE. THE BUILDING MATERIAL IS GALVANIZED STEEL. THE PHOTOGRAPH WAS TAKEN WITH A 4X5 VIEW CAMERA ON TUNGSTEN FILM UNDER DAYLIGHT TO LESSEN CONTRAST. (USA)

■ 221 FROM THE ANNUAL REPORT OF THE CHICAGO BOARD OF TRADE. AS THE DESIGNERS WANTED A 40'S LOOK, BLACK-AND-WHITE WAS DECIDED UPON. IT WAS TAKEN FROM THE 23RD FLOOR LEDGE OF A NEARBY BUILDING AT 3.45 PM IN WINTER WHEN DUSK CAME AND THE RATIO BETWEEN THE AVAILABLE LIGHT, THE BUILDING LIGHTS, AND THE INSIDE LIGHT ARRIVED AT THE RIGHT POINT. (USA)

● 219 AUFNAHME DER EMPFANGSHALLE IM SOLANA-IBM ZENTRUM. DIE WICHTIGSTE LICHTQUELLE WAR NATÜRLICHES LICHT. DIE GESTALT IM EINGANG GIBT EINE VORSTELLUNG VOM GRÖSSENVERHÄLTNIS. (USA)

● 220 DETAILAUFNAHME EINES MÖBELFABRIK-GEBÄUDES VON HERMAN MILLER. DAS BAUMATERIAL WAR GALVANISIERTER STAHL. ES WURDE EIN AUF TAGESLICHT EINGESTELLTER TUNGSTENFILM VERWENDET, UM DEN KONTRAST ZU MILDERN. (USA)

● 221 AUS EINEM JAHRESBERICHT FÜR DIE HANDELSKAMMER VON CHICAGO. DIE AUFNAHME WURDE VOM FENSTERSIMS DES 23STEN STOCKWERKS EINES BENACHBARTEN GEBÄUDES AUS GEMACHT UND ZWAR UM 15.45 UHR IM WINTER, ALS DIE DÄMMERUNG EINSETZTE UND DAS ZUSAMMENSPIEL VON NATÜRLICHEM LICHT UND DER AUSSEN- UND INNENBELEUCHTUNG GENAU RICHTIG WAR. (USA)

▲ 219 PHOTO DU HALL D'ENTRÉE DU CENTRE SOLANA-IBM. LE PHOTOGRAPHE A SURTOUT UTILISÉ UN ÉCLAIRAGE NATUREL. LA FIGURE QUI APPARAÎT À L'ENTRÉE DONNE UNE IDÉE DE L'ÉCHELLE. (USA)

▲ 220 PHOTO DE DÉTAIL DE L'USINE OÙ SONT FABRIQUÉS LES MEUBLES HERMANN MILLER, CONSTRUITE EN ACIER GALVANISÉ. LA PHOTO A ÉTÉ RÉALISÉE AVEC UN APPAREIL 4X5 ET UNE PELLICULE AU TUNGSTÈNE RÉGLÉE SUR LUMIÈRE NATURELLE. (USA)

▲ 221 D'UN RAPPORT ANNUEL DE LA CHAMBRE DE COMMERCE DE CHICAGO. LA PHOTO A ÉTÉ PRISE EN HIVER, DANS L'APRÈS-MIDI, VERS 15 H 45; LE PHOTOGRAPHE A PROFITÉ AINSI DES EFFETS COMBINÉS D'UNE LUMIÈRE NATURELLE ET D'UN ÉCLAIRAGE ÉLECTRIQUE. POUR LA PHOTO, IL S'ÉTAIT POSTÉ JUSTE SUR LE REBORD D'UNE FENÊTRE, AU 23E ÉTAGE DU BÂTIMENT VOISIN. (USA)

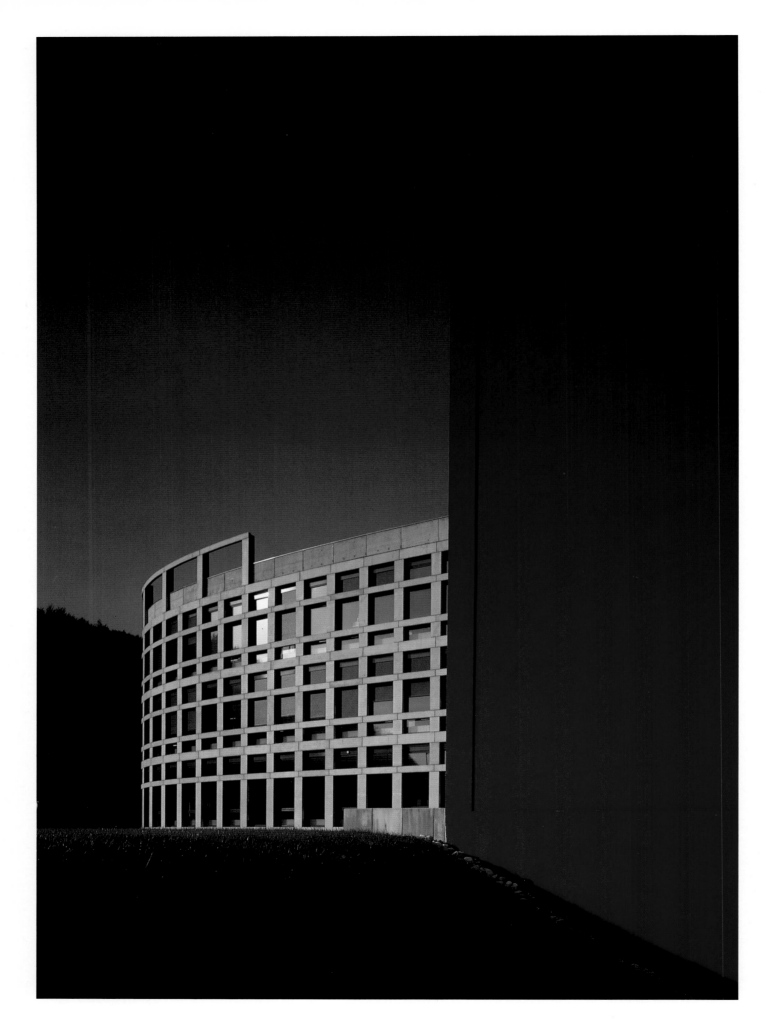

PHOTOGRAPHER:

JOSEF PAUSCH

CAMERA:

LINHOF 4X5

FILM:

KODAK EKTACHROME

ART DIRECTOR:

FRANZ HOCHWARTER

DESIGNER:

SYLVIA DANZINGER

AGENCY:

DEMNER & MERLICEK

< 222

PHOTOGRAPHER:

CRAIG CUTLER

REPRESENTATIVE:

MARZENA

CAMERA:

MAMIYA RZ 6X7

FILM:

TMX

CLIENT:

BELL ATLANTIC

ART DIRECTOR:

DOMINGO PEREZ

AGENCY:

J. WALTER THOMPSON

223

■ 222 PHOTOGRAPH (WITH WIDE-ANGLE LENS) OF THE HEADQUARTERS OF ONE OF AUSTRIA'S LEADING FURNITURE MANUFACTURERS. (AUT)

■ 223 THE BELL ATLANTIC HEADQUARTERS IN PHILADELPHIA. THE PHOTOGRAPH, ADVERTISING THINK SOFTWARE, WAS ASSIGNED TO SHOW THAT THERE ARE ALTERNATIVE WAYS OF ENVISIONING OBJECTS AS OPPOSED TO SEEING ONLY THE OBVIOUS. (USA)

● 222 AUFNAHME (MIT WEITWINKELOBJEKTIV) DES FIRMENSITZES EINES DER FÜHRENDEN MÖBELHERSTELLER ÖSTERREICHS. (AUT)

● 223 DER BELL ATLANTIC FIRMENSITZ IN PHILADELPHIA. DIE AUFNAHME, FÜR THINK-SOFTWARE-WERBUNG VERWENDET, SOLLTE ZEIGEN, DASS ES ANDERE WEGE GIBT, DIE DINGE ZU SEHEN, MEHR ALS NUR DIE OFFEN-SICHTLICHEN. (USA)

▲ 222 PHOTO (PRISE AU TÉLÉOBJECTIF) DU SIÈGE DE LA FIRME D'UN DES PRINCIPAUX FABRICANTS DE MEUBLES D'AUTRICHE. (AUT)

▲ 223 LE SIÈGE DE LA FIRME BELL ATLANTIC À PHILADELPHIE. LA PHOTO, UTILISÉE DANS LA PUBLICITÉ POUR THINK SOFTWARE, DE-VAIT MONTRER QU'IL EXISTE D'AUTRES MOYENS DE VOIR LES CHOSES, DERRIÈRE LEUR ASPECT IMMÉDIAT. (USA)

WILDLIFE

TIERE

ANIMAUX

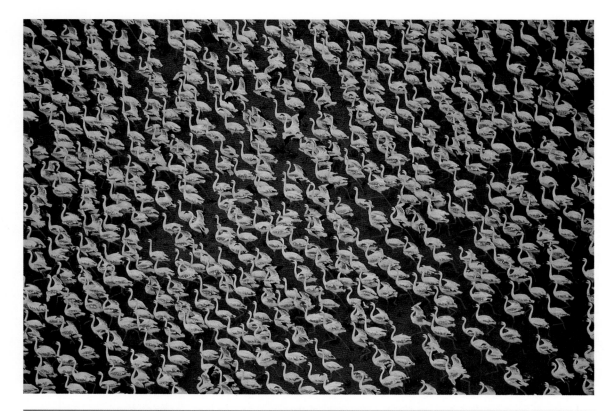

(FIRST PAGE OF
WILDLIFE SECTION)
PHOTOGRAPHER:
TEIJI SAGA
REPRESENTATIVES:
ALLSTOCK (USA)
PACIFIC PRESS
SERVICE (JPN)

PUBLISHER:
WM. C. BROWN
PUBLISHERS
ART DIRECTOR:
FAYE SCHILLING
DESIGNER:
MARK E.
CHRISTIANSON
< 224

PHOTOGRAPHER:
FRANS LANTING
PUBLISHER:
NATIONAL GEOGRAPHIC
225, 226

PHOTOGRAPHER:

DIETER BLUM

CAMERA:

LEICA R5

FILM:

KODAK

EKTACHROME 100

CLIENT:

IBM DEUTSCHLAND

ART DIRECTORS:

DIETER BLUM,

HERBERT SUHR

DESIGNER:

HERBERT SUHR

227

■ 224 (FIRST PAGE OF WILD LIFE SECTION) A WHOOPER SWAN PHOTOGRAPHED BY TEIJI SAGA. SAGA SPENDS FIVE MONTHS A YEAR WITH THIS MIGRATORY BIRD THAT COMES FROM SIBERIA TO JAPAN. (USA)

■ 225, 226 THESE PHOTOGRAPHS FOR NATIONAL GEOGRAPHIC WERE TAKEN BY FRANS LANTING, A FAMOUS NATURE PHOTOGRAPHER. SHOWN ARE FLAMINGOS, PHOTOGRAPHED IN BOTSWANA, AND A BLACK EGRET FISHING IN THE OKAVANGO. IT IS FANNING OUT ITS WINGS TO SHADE THE WATER FROM GLARE. AMONG THE MANY AWARDS MR. LANTING RECEIVED IS THE "BBC WILDLIFE PHOTOGRAPHER OF THE YEAR 1991." (USA)

■ 227 RHINOS FROM EAST AFRICA. PHOTOGRAPHED IN A GERMAN ZOO FOR AN IBM IN-HOUSE PUBLICATION. (GER)

● 224 (ERSTE SEITE) EIN SINGSCHWAN, PHOTOGRAPHIERT VON TEIJI SAGA, DER FÜNF MONATE IM JAHR MIT IHNEN VERBRINGT, WENN DIESE ZUGVÖGEL VON SIBIRIEN NACH JAPAN KOMMEN. (USA)

● 225, 226 AUFNAHMEN VON FRANS LANTING FÜR NATIONAL GEOGRAPHIC. ER GEHÖRT ZU DEN BEKANNTESTEN NATURPHOTOGRAPHEN. DIE FLAMINGOS PHOTOGRAPHIERTE ER IN BOTSWANA, DEN SCHWARZEN REIHER AM OKA-VANGO-FLUSS. DIESER HAT EINE SPEZIELLE FISCHTECHNIK: DIE AUSGEBREITETEN FLÜGEL WERFEN SCHATTEN AUF DAS WASSER. FRANS LANTING WURDE U.A. ZUM «BBC WILDLIFE PHOTOGRAPHER 1991» GEWÄHLT. (USA)

● 227 SPITZMAULNASHÖRNER AUS OSTAFRI-KA, IN EINEM DEUTSCHEN ZOO FÜR EINE IBM-FIRMENPUBLIKATION AUFGENOMMEN. (GER)

▲ 224 (PREMIÈRE PAGE) UN CYGNE CHAN-TEUR, PHOTOGRAPHIÉ PAR TEIJI SAGA. IL PASSE CINQ MOIS PAR AN AUPRÈS DE CES OI-SEAUX MIGRATEURS DE SIBÉRIE LORSQU'ILS VIENNENT AU JAPON. (USA)

▲ 225, 226 PHOTOS DE FRANS LANTING, L'UN DES PLUS CÉLÈBRES PHOTOGRAPHES DE LA NATURE, POUR NATIONAL GEOGRAPHIC. LES FLAMANTS ONT ÉTÉ PRIS AU BOTSWANA ET LE HÉRON CENDRÉ SUR LE FLEUVE OKAVANGO. CET OISEAU A UNE TECHNIQUE DE PÊCHE PARTICLULIÈRE: SES AILES DÉPLOYÉES LUI PERMETTENT DE FAIRE DE L'OMBRE SUR L'EAU. FRANS LANTING A ÉTÉ NOMMÉ PHOTO-GRAPHE «BBC WILDLIFE» 1991. (USA)

▲ 227 DES RHINOCÉROS DE L'EST DE L'AFRI-QUE, PHOTOGRAPHIÉS DANS UN ZOO ALLE-MAND POUR UNE PUBLICATION D'IBM. (GER)

PHOTOGRAPHER:

DIRK FISCHER

CAMERA:

NIKON FE2

FILM:

TRI-X 800

228

■ 228 FROM A SELF-ASSIGNED SERIES ON ANIMALS IN ZOOS. THESE ELEPHANTS WERE PHOTOGRAPHED IN THE PALE LIGHT OF THE EVENING THROUGH THE GLASS ROOF OF THEIR HOUSE. (USA)

■ 229 PHOTOGRAPHER JOHN RUNNING WENT OUT WITH A MEXICAN FISHING FAMILY PRIMA- RILY FISHING FOR SHARK IN THE SEA OF CORTEZ. ONE MORNING, THEY CAUGHT THIS ONE. THE PHOTOGRAPH APPEARED IN THE BOOK *PICTURES FOR SOLOMON.* (USA)

■ 230 THIS PHOTOGRAPH IS AN OUT-TAKE FROM AN AD CAMPAIGN FOR CHEVRON CHEMI- CAL CO., WHO WANTED TO SHOW THE DAN- GERS OF WORKING IN THE OIL FIELDS OF SOUTHWEST USA. AS THE SNAKE (WESTERN DIAMOND BACK, A DEADLY RATTLESNAKE) WAS ALIVE, THREE ANIMAL TRAINERS WERE HIRED TO CONTROL IT. A DESERT SET WITH DUMMY LEGS (NOBODY WOULD STAND IN FOR THIS JOB), OLD BOOTS AND PANTS WERE SET UP IN THE STUDIO. (USA)

● 228 AUS EINER FREIEN PHOTOREIHE ZUM THEMA TIERE IM ZOO. DIESE ELEFANTEN WURDEN IM FAHLEN LICHT DES FRÜHEN ABENDS DURCH DAS GLASDACH DES ELEFAN- TENHAUSES PHOTOGRAPHIERT. (USA)

● 229 DER PHOTOGRAPH JOHN RUNNING BEGLEITETE EINE MEXIKANISCHE FISCHER- FAMILIE, DIE HAUPTSÄCHLICH HAIE FÄNGT. DIESES EXEMPLAR GING EINES MORGENS IN NETZ. DIE AUFNAHME WURDE IN EINEM BUCH VERÖFFENTLICHT. (USA)

● 230 DIESE AUFNAHME ENTSTAND IM RAH- MEN EINER SERIE FÜR EINE WERBEKAMPAGNE DER FIRMA CHEVRON CHEMICAL, DIE DIE GEFAHREN BEI DER ARBEIT IN DEN ÖLFEL- DERN IM SÜDWESTEN DER USA ZEIGEN WOLL- TE. DIE KLAPPERSCHLANGE, DEREN GIFT TÖDLICH IST, WAR LEBENDIG UND MUSSTE VON DREI DOMPTEUREN IN SCHACH GEHALTEN WERDEN. DIE WÜSTENDEKORATION MIT EINER PUPPE ANSTELLE EINES LEBENDIGEN MO- DELLS WURDE IM STUDIO AUFGEBAUT. (USA)

▲ 228 D'UNE SÉRIE SUR LE THÈME DES ANI- MAUX DANS LES ZOOS. CES PACHYDERMES ONT ÉTÉ PHOTOGRAPHIÉS DANS LA LUMIÈRE DU CRÉPUSCULE, AU TRAVERS DE LA VER- RIÈRE DE LA MAISON DES ÉLÉPHANTS. (GER)

▲ 229 LE PHOTOGRAPHE PUT ACCOMPAGNER UNE FAMILLE DE PÊCHEURS MEXICAINS QUI ATTRAPENT SURTOUT DES REQUINS. UN MATIN, ILS PRIRENT CE SPÉCIMEN DANS LEURS FILETS. LA PHOTO A ÉTÉ PUBLIÉE DANS UN LIVRE. (USA)

▲ 230 PHOTO POUR UNE CAMPAGNE DE LA FIRME CHEVRON CHEMICAL: ON Y MONTRE LES DANGERS QU'ENCOURENT CEUX QUI TRA- VAILLENT DANS LES PUITS DE PÉTROLE DU SUD-OUEST DES ÉTATS-UNIS. LE SERPENT À SONNETTES, DONT LA MORSURE EST MOR- TELLE, ÉTAIT BIEN VIVANT: IL FALLUT TROIS DOMPTEURS POUR LE TENIR EN RESPECT. LE DÉCOR DU DÉSERT A ÉTÉ CONSTRUIT EN STU- DIO: UN MANNEQUIN A ÉTÉ REVÊTU DU JEANS ET DE VIEILLES CHAUSSURES. (USA)

PHOTOGRAPHER:
JOHN RUNNING
PUBLISHER:
NORTHLAND
PUBLISHING
DESIGNER:
DAVID JENNY
229

PHOTOGRAPHER:
STEVE FUKUDA
CAMERA:
SINAR
FILM:
FUJI
CLIENT:
CHEVRON CHEM-
ICAL CO.

ART DIRECTOR:
DAVE DEVENCENZI
DESIGNER:
RICK SAMS
AGENCY:
BRIDGE COMMUNICA-
TION ADVERTISING
230

SPORTS

SPORT

SPORT

(FIRST PAGE OF
SPORTS SECTION)
PHOTOGRAPHER:
LEN RUBENSTEIN
CAMERA:
NIKON F4
FILM:
AGFA 1000, KODAK
RECORDING
CLIENT:
BABSON COLLEGE
ART DIRECTOR:
MARK FORD
HAND COLORATION:
JEAN BAILEY
< 231

PHOTOGRAPHER:
LACI PERÉNYI
CAMERA:
NIKONOS 5
PUBLISHER:
SPORTS
GRUNER & JAHR
ART DIRECTOR:
MICHAEL RABANUS
232

PHOTOGRAPHERS:
CHARLES COMPÈRE,
THOMAS ZIMMERMANN
CLIENT:
KLÖCKNER-HUMBOLDT-
DEUTZ AG
ART DIRECTOR:
PETER HOLZHAUSEN
DESIGNER:
PETER HOLZHAUSEN
AGENCY:
HOLZHAUSEN WERBE-
AGENTUR GMBH
> 233

■ **231** (FIRST PAGE OF SPORTS SECTION) AN INTERPRETATION OF THE NEW SWIMMING POOL OF BRESSON COLLEGE. THE ORIGINAL PHOTOGRAPH WAS TAKEN AT NIGHT WITH ALL AVAILABLE LIGHT. THE LENS WAS INTENTION-ALLY FOGGED. A PRINT WAS THEN HAND-COL-ORED, RELIT AND REPHOTOGRAPHED TO OB-TAIN THE FINAL IMAGE. (USA)

■ **232** PHOTOGRAPHER LACI PERÉNYI, HIM-SELF A FORMER MEMBER OF THE GERMAN NATIONAL SWIMMING TEAM AND THEREFORE EXPERT IN THIS FIELD, TOOK THIS PHOTO-GRAPH WITH A NIKONOS 5 FOR A FEATURE IN *SPORTS* MAGAZINE. (GER)

■ **233** THIS PHOTOGRAPH WAS USED IN A CAL-ENDAR FOR DEUTZ MOTOR COMPANY TO SHOW HOW MAN (AND A MACHINE) TURNS ENERGY INTO OUTPUT. (GER)

● **231** (ERSTE SEITE) INTERPRETATION DES NEUEN SWIMMINGPOOLS EINES COLLEGES. DIE URSPRÜNGLICHE AUFNAHME ENTSTAND NACHTS MIT DEM VORHANDENEN LICHT. DAS OBJEKTIV WURDE ABSICHTLICH BENEBELT, DER ABZUG HANDKOLORIERT, NOCHMALS BELEUCHTET UND PHOTOGRAPHIERT, UM DAS GEWÜNSCHTE RESULT ZU ERHALTEN. (USA)

● **232** DER PHOTOGRAPH LACI PERÉNYI, ALS EHEMALIGES MITGLIED DER DEUTSCHEN NA-TIONALMANNSCHAFT IM SCHWIMMEN EXPERTE IN DIESEM BEREICH, PHOTOGRAPHIERTE MIT EINER NIKONOS 5 IM AUFTRAG DER ZEIT-SCHRIFT *SPORTS*. (GER)

● **233** DIE AUFNAHMEN DES KALENDERS FÜR DEUTZ MOTOR SOLLTEN AUSDRÜCKEN, WIE DER MENSCH (UND DIE MASCHINE) ENERGIE IN LEISTUNG UMSETZT. (GER)

▲ **231** (PREMIÈRE PAGE) LA NOUVELLE PISCINE D'UN COLLÈGE. UNE PREMIÈRE PHOTO FUT PRISE DE NUIT AVEC L'ÉCLAIRAGE DISPONIBLE. C'EST INTENTIONNELLEMENT QUE LA PHOTO A ÉTÉ VOILÉE. LE TIRAGE A ÉTÉ ENSUITE COLORÉ MAIN, ÉCLAIRÉ ET PHO-TOGRAPHIÉ ENCORE UNE FOIS, AFIN D'OB-TENIR LE RÉSULTAT FINAL. (USA)

▲ **232** LE PHOTOGRAPHE LACI PERÉNYI, EX-PERT EN NATATION EN SA QUALITÉ D'ANCIEN MEMBRE DE L'ÉQUIPE NATIONALE ALLEMANDE, A RÉALISÉ CETTE PHOTO À LA DEMANDE DU MAGAZINE *SPORTS*; IL A TRAVAILLÉ AVEC UN APPAREIL NIKONOS 5. (GER)

▲ **233** LES PHOTOS DE CE CALENDRIER POUR DEUTZ MOTOR DEVAIENT SUGGÉRER COMMENT L'HOMME (ET LA MACHINE) TRANSPOSE L'ÉNERGIE EN PERFORMANCE. (GER)

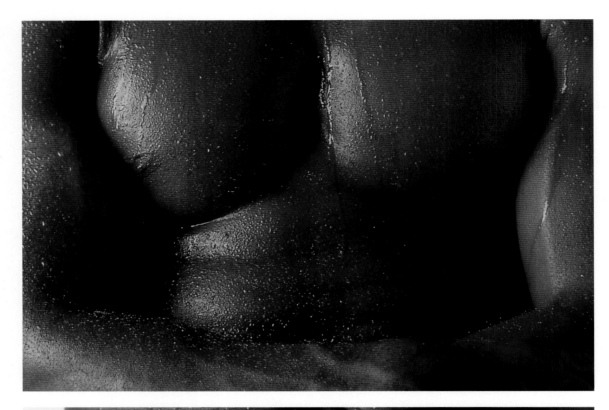

PHOTOGRAPHER: DESIGNER:
ROBERT MIZONO   NEIL SHAKERY
CLIENT: AGENCY:
MIRAGE HOTEL   HAL RINEY
ART DIRECTORS: & PARTNERS
TOM TIECHE,   234-236
BEN WONG

■ 234-236 PORTRAITS OF HEAVYWEIGHT   ● 234-236 PORTRÄTS DER SCHWERGEWICHT-   ▲ 234-236 PORTRAITS DES CHAMPIONS DE
CHAMPION BOXERS BUSTER DOUGLASS AND   BOX-CHAMPIONS BUSTER DOUGLASS UND   BOXE CATÉGORIE POIDS LOURD, BUSTER
EVANDER HOLYFIELD. (USA)   EVANDER HOLYFIELD. (USA)   DOUGLASS ET EVANDER HOLYFIELD. (USA)

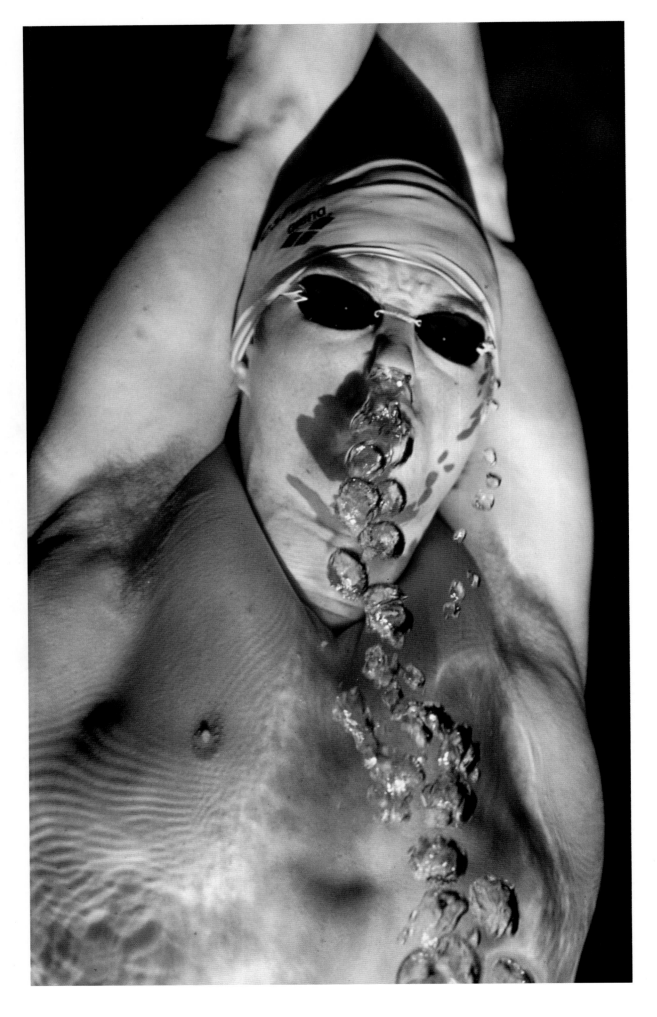

PHOTOGRAPHER:

LACI PERÉNYI

CAMERA:

NIKONOS 5

PUBLISHER:

SPORTS

GRUNER & JAHR

ART DIRECTOR:

MICHAEL RABANUS

< 237

PHOTOGRAPHERS:

CHARLES COMPÈRE,

THOMAS ZIMMERMANN

CLIENT:

KLÖCKNER-HUMBOLDT-

DEUTZ AG

ART DIRECTOR:

PETER HOLZHAUSEN

DESIGNER:

PETER HOLZHAUSEN

AGENCY:

HOLZHAUSEN WERBE-

AGENTUR GMBH

238

■ 237 FOR MANY YEARS PHOTOGRAPHER LACI PERÉNYI WAS IN THE GERMAN NATIONAL SWIMMING TEAM. HE KNOWS WHICH WAY THE BUBBLES WILL GO AND CAN ANTICIPATE THE RIGHT MOMENT TO PRESS THE TRIGGER. THIS PHOTOGRAPH, AN ASSIGNMENT FOR *SPORTS* MAGAZINE, WAS TAKEN WITH A NIKONOS 5 AND AN UNDERWATER FLASHLIGHT. (GER)

● 237 JAHRELANG GEHÖRTE DER PHOTO-GRAPH LACI PERÉNYI ZUM DEUTSCHEN NATIO-NALSCHWIMM-TEAM. ER KANN DIE BLASEN-BILDUNG EINSCHÄTZEN, WEISS, WANN DER RICHTIGE MOMENT GEKOMMEN IST. DIESE AUFNAHME WURDE IM AUFTRAG DER ZEIT-SCHRIFT *SPORTS* GEMACHT, UND ZWAR MIT UNTERWASSERBLITZ. (GER)

▲ 237 PENDANT DES ANNÉES, LE PHOTO-GRAPHE LACI PERÉNYI A FAIT PARTIE DE L'ÉQUIPE NATIONALE ALLEMANDE DE NATA-TION. IL SAIT DONC QUEL SERA LE MOMENT PROPICE POUR LA PHOTO. CETTE DERNIÈRE A ÉTÉ RÉALISÉ POUR LE MAGAZINE *SPORTS*, AVEC UN FLASH SPÉCIAL POUR LA PHOTO SOUS-MARINE. (GER)

■ 238 THE ASSIGNMENT FOR THIS PHOTO-GRAPH USED IN THE CALENDAR OF AN AUTO-MOBILE COMPANY WAS TO SHOW THE INTER-RELATION OF QUALITY AND OUTPUT OF PER-FORMANCE. (GER)

● 238 DIESE AUFNAHME, DIE IN EINEN KALEN-DER EINES MOTORENHERSTELLERS VERWEN-DET WURDE, SOLLTE DEN ZUSAMMENHANG VON QUALITÄT UND LEISTUNG DARSTELLEN. SPORT WAR DESHALB DAS THEMA. (GER)

▲ 238 CETTE PHOTO QUI A ÉTÉ REPRODUITE SUR LE CALENDRIER D'UN FABRICANT DE MOTEURS DEVAIT MONTRER LA RELATION ENTRE LA QUALITÉ ET LA PERFORMANCE. LE THÈME EN ÉTAIT DONC LE SPORT. (GER)

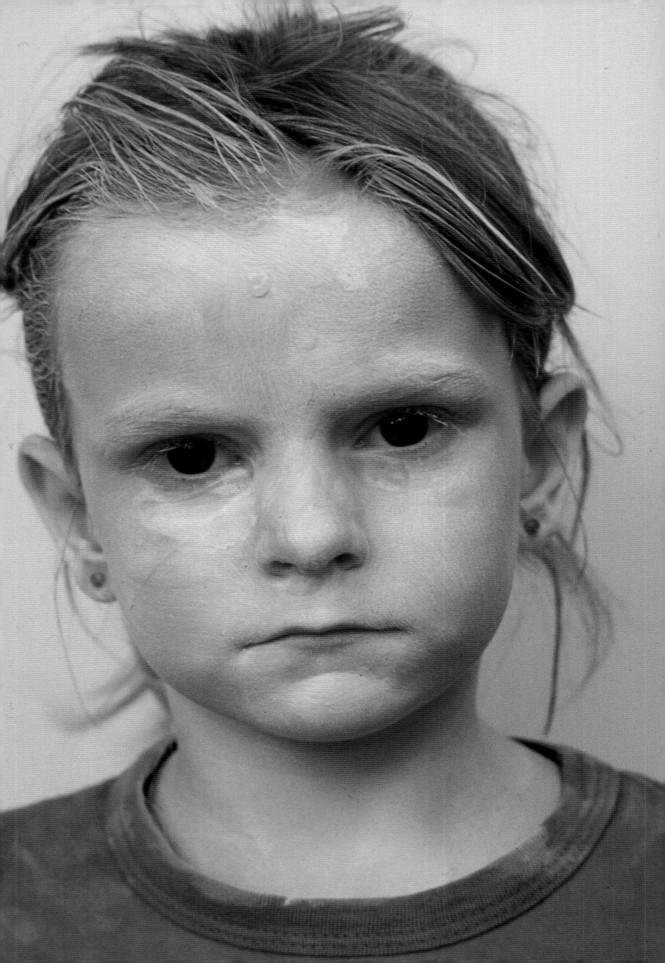

FINE ART

KUNST

ART

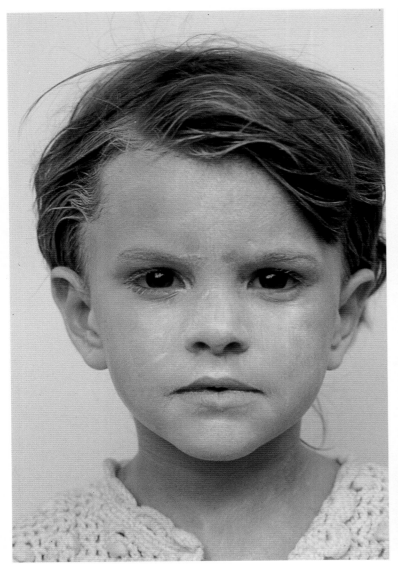 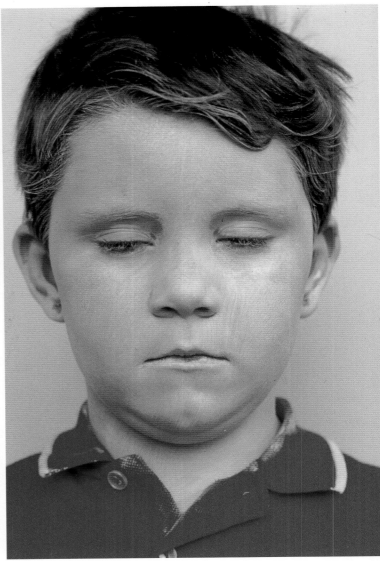

(FIRST PAGE OF FINE
ART SECTION AND
THIS DOUBLE SPREAD)
PHOTOGRAPHER:
GOTTFRIED HELNWEIN
ART DIRECTOR:
GOTTFRIED HELNWEIN
239-243

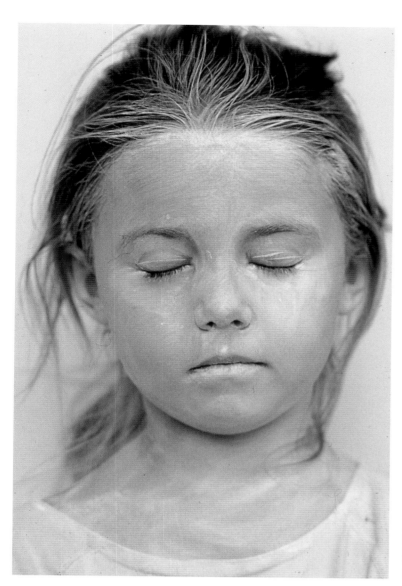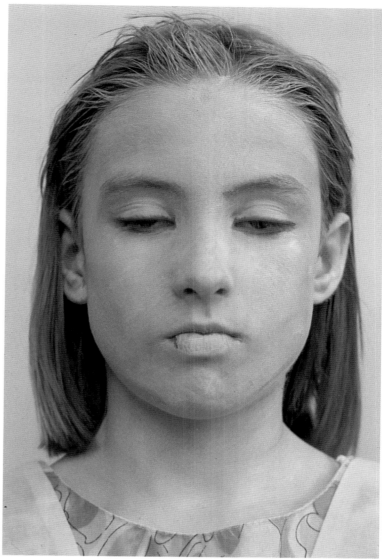

■ 239-243 (FIRST PAGE OF FINE ART SECTION AND THIS DOUBLE SPREAD) "THE NIGHT OF 9TH NOVEMBER." THIS SERIES IS PART OF A 100 M-LONG INSTALLATION ERECTED IN FRONT OF THE LUDWIG MUSEUM IN COLOGNE DURING THE PHOTOKINA TRADE SHOW IN COMMEMORATION OF CRYSTAL NIGHT (9TH/10TH NOVEMBER 1938), DURING WHICH THE NAZIS RAMPAGED THROUGHOUT GERMANY, BURNING SYNAGOGUES AND BREAKING THE WINDOWS OF JEWISH SCHOOLS, HOMES AND SHOPS. (GER)

● 239-243 (ERSTE SEITE UND DIESE DOPPELSEITE) »NEUNTER NOVEMBER NACHT« – AUFNAHMEN AUS EINEM KUNSTPROJEKT VON GOTTFRIED HELNWEIN IN FORM EINER 100 M LANGEN INSTALLATION VOR DEM MUSEUM LUDWIG IN KÖLN WÄHREND DER PHOTOKINA. SIE SOLLTE AN DIE REICHSKRISTALLNACHT ERINNERN, DIE NACHT VOM 9. AUF DEN 10. NOVEMBER 1938, IN DER DIE NAZIS SYNAGOGEN, JÜDISCHE FRIEDHÖFE UND WOHN- UND GESCHÄFTSHÄUSER ZERSTÖRTEN. (GER).

▲ 239-243 (PREMIÈRE PAGE ET CETTE DOUBLE PAGE) «LA NUIT DU 9 NOVEMBRE». SÉRIE DE PHOTOS DE GOTTFRIED HELNWEIN FAISANT PARTIE D'UNE INSTALLATION DE 100 M DE LONG, PRÉSENTÉE DEVANT LE MUSÉE LUDWIG DE COLOGNE À L'OCCASION DE LA PHOTOKINA. ELLE RAPPELLE LA TRAGIQUE NUIT DE CRISTAL,.DU 9 AU 10 NOVEMBRE 1938, AU COURS DE LAQUELLE LES NAZIS DÉTRUISIRENT LES SYNAGOGUES, LES CIMETIÈRES ET LES MAGASINS JUIFS. (GER)

PHOTOGRAPHER:

HANS NELEMAN

REPRESENTATIVE:

NELEMAN STUDIO

CAMERA:

SINAR P 8X10

FILM:

KODAK EKTACHROME 64

CLIENT:

DAYTON HUDSON

ART DIRECTOR:

BILL THORBURN

STYLIST:

PAMELA NEEDLES

AGENCY:

DAYTON HUDSON/

IN-HOUSE

< 244

PHOTOGRAPHER:

GEORGE SIMHONI

REPRESENTATIVES:

ROBIN DICTENBERG (USA),

DAVID GARDINER (GBR),

WESTSIDE STUDIO (CAN)

CAMERA:

HASSELBLAD

FILM:

EKTACHROME 400

BACKDROP:

KELVIN BRITTON

MAKE-UP:

NANCY SIMHONI

245

■ 244 THIS PHOTOGRAPH IS THE RESULT OF A CARTE BLANCHE ASSIGNMENT FROM DAYTON HUDSON DEPARTMENT STORE FOR THEIR CHRISTMAS ADVERTISING, WHICH WAS MEANT TO PROMOTE JOY AND PEACE. (USA)

■ 245 A FREE STUDY USED AS SELF-PROMO-TION BY THE PHOTOGRAPHER. (CAN)

● 244 BEI DIESER AUFNAHME FÜR DIE WEIH-NACHTSWERBUNG DES KAUFHAUSES DAYTON HUDSON HATTE DER PHOTOGRAPH VÖLLIG FREIE HAND. ES GING EINFACH DARUM, WEIH-NACHTSSTIMMUNG ZU VERBREITEN. (USA)

● 245 FREIE STUDIE DES PHOTOGRAPHEN, ALS EIGENWERBUNG VERWENDET. (CAN)

▲ 244 LE PHOTOGRAPHE AVAIT REÇU CARTE BLANCHE POUR LA PUBLICITÉ DE NOËL DU MAGASIN DAYTON HUDSON: IL LUI AVAIT ÉTÉ SIMPLEMENT DEMANDÉ D'EXPRIMER LA JOIE ET LA PAIX DE CETTE FÊTE. (USA)

▲ 245 ÉTUDE LIBRE, UTILISÉE À DES FINS AUTOPROMOTIONNELLES. (CAN)

PHOTOGRAPHER:

JAN OSWALD

CAMERA:

SINAR P 4X5

FILM:

KODAK EKTACHROME 64

ART DIRECTOR:

JAN OSWALD

STUDIO:

JAN OSWALD PHOTO-

GRAPHY

246, 247

PHOTOGRAPHER:

NADAV KANDER

ART DIRECTOR:

LEE RIPPER

DESIGNERS:

JOHN GORHAM,

NADAV KANDER

> 248

■ **246, 247** BLACK-AND-WHITE PRINTS MIXED IN A COLOR COLLAGE PLAYING ON THE NOTION OF PHOTOGRAPHY AS A TWO-DIMENSIONAL REPRESENTATION OF A THREE-DIMENSIONAL REALITY. THE BACKGROUNDS WERE PAINTED BY THE PHOTOGRAPHER. "STATE OF THE ARTIST II" CONCERNS THE CREATIVE ACT, "SUBTLE EFFECTS" REFERS TO THE CONTEMPORARY FEELING OF BEING TRAPPED BY THE PATRIARCHAL SYSTEM. (USA)

■ **248** "LEGS," ANOTHER SIDE OF BRITISH PHOTOGRAPHER NADAV KANDER WHO BECAME FAMOUS MAINLY THROUGH HIS LANDSCAPE PHOTOGRAPHY. (GBR)

● **246, 247** SCHWARZWEISSPHOTOS IN EINER FARBCOLLAGE, EINE ANSPIELUNG AUF DAS ZWEIDIMENSIONALE MEDIUM, DAS DIE DREIDIMENSIONALE REALITÄT WIEDERGIBT. DER HINTERGRUND WURDE VOM PHOTOGRAPHEN GEMALT. «STATE OF THE ARTIST II» BEFASST SICH MIT DEM KREATIVEN AKT; «SUBTLE EFFECTS» SYMBOLISIERT DAS GEFÜHL DER UNTERDRÜCKUNG IM GEGENWÄRTIGEN PATRIARCHALISCHEN SYSTEM. (USA)

● **248** «LEGS», EINE ANDERE SEITE DES VOR ALLEM DURCH SEINE LANDSCHAFTSAUFNAHMEN BEKANNT GEWORDENEN PHOTOGRAPHEN NADAV KANDER. (GBR)

▲ **246, 247** PORTRAITS DU PHOTOGRAPHE, QUI ASSOCIENT DES TIRAGES SUR PAPIER EN NOIR ET BLANC ET DES ÉLÉMENTS EN COULEURS: «STATE OF THE ARTIST II» ÉVOQUE LE PASSAGE À L'ACTE CRÉATIF, ET «SUBTLE EFFECTS» SYMBOLISE LE SENTIMENT D'OPPRESSION DEVANT LE SYSTÈME PATRIARÇAL ACTUEL. LE PREMIER PORTRAIT EST EN PARTIE RECOUVERT DE CENDRE; LES FONDS ONT ÉTÉ PEINTS PAR LE PHOTOGRAPHE. (USA)

▲ **248** «LEGS»: UNE NOUVELLE FACETTE DU CÉLÈBRE PHOTOGRAPHE NADAV KANDER, SURTOUT CONNU POUR SES PHOTOS DE PAYSAGES. (GBR)

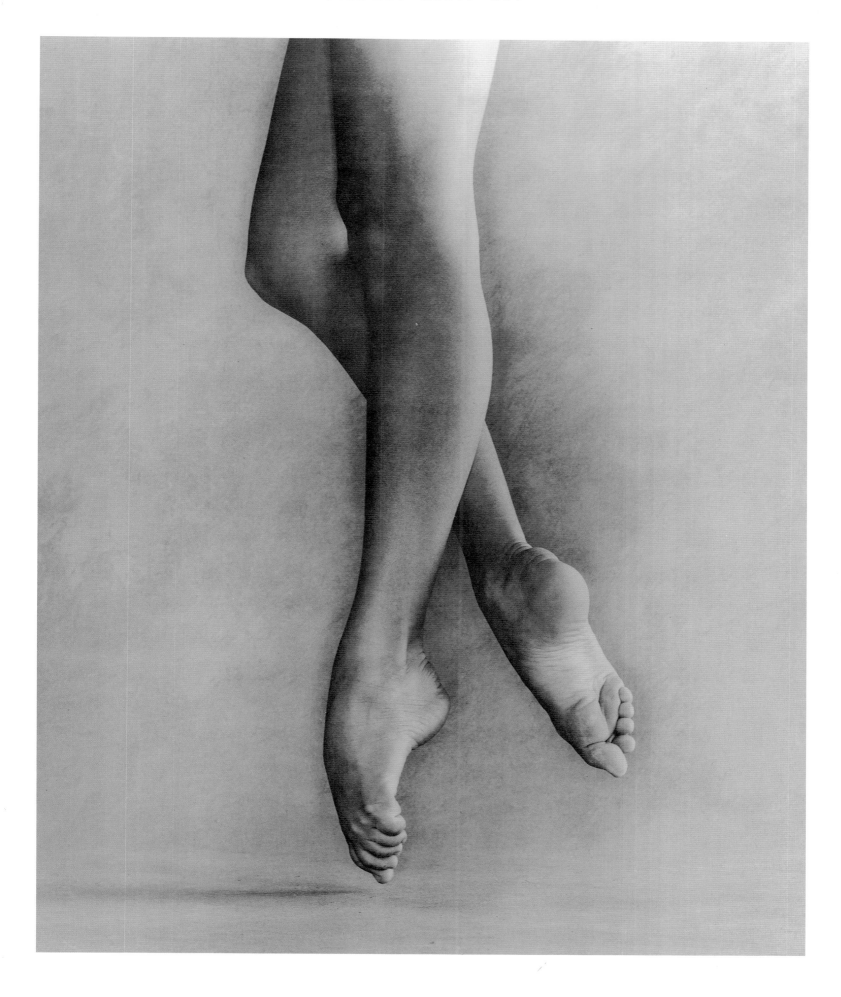

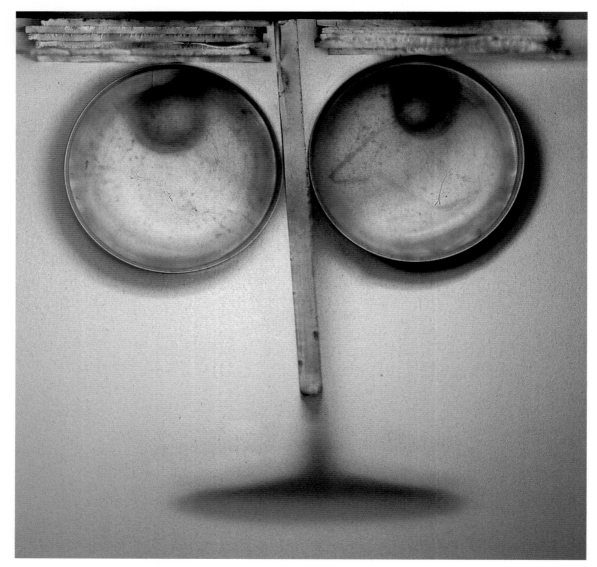

PHOTOGRAPHER:

ZAFER BARAN

ART DIRECTOR:

ALAN FLETCHER

DESIGNER:

QUENTIN NEWARK

AGENCY:

PENTAGRAM

DESIGN LTD.

249-253

■ 249-253 PHOTOGRAPHS FROM A SELF-PRO-MOTIONAL BOOK OF COMMISSIONED AND NON-COMMISSIONED PHOTOGRAPHS BY ZAFER BARAN. THE "FACE" PHOTOGRAPH IS AN UP-SIDE-DOWN STILL LIFE. (GBR)

● 249-253 AUFNAHMEN AUS EINER EIGENWER-BUNGSBROSCHÜRE MIT AUFTRAGS- UND FREI-ER PHOTOGRAPHIE VON ZAFER BARAN. DAS «GESICHT» IST EIN AUF DEN KOPF GESTELL-TES STILLEBEN. (GBR)

▲ 249-253 D'UNE BROCHURE AUTOPROMO-TIONNELLE COMPORTANT DES PHOTOS DE COMMANDE ET DES ÉTUDES LIBRES DE ZAFER BARAN. LE «VISAGE» EST UNE NATURE MORTE VUE À L'ENVERS. (GBR)

PHOTOGRAPHERS:

MAX JACOT,

JULIE SAUTER

CAMERA:

PENTAX 645

FILM:

T-MAX 400, T-MAX 100

PUBLISHER:

EDITIONS OLIZANE

254

PHOTOGRAPHER:

ELLE SCHUSTER

CAMERA:

SINAR 4X5

FILM:

KODAK EKTACHROME 64

DAYLIGHT 4X5

CLIENT:

JAMES RIVER PREMIUM

PRINTING PAPERS

DESIGNER:

REX PETEET

AGENCY:

SIBLEY PETEET DESIGN

> 255

■ 254 "THE HEADER" (ST. SAPHORIN, SWIT-ZERLAND), THIS IMAGE IS PART OF AN EXTEN-SIVE SERIES ON SWITZERLAND SHOWING THE QUALITIES OF A MONTAGE TECHNIQUE, PUB-LISHED IN A BOOK. (SWI)

■ 255 THIS PHOTOGRAPH SERVED AS COVER OF A PAPER SAMPLE BROCHURE. THE ASSIGN-MENT WAS TO COMBINE BLACK-AND-WHITE AND COLOR PHOTOGRAPHY WITH A PAINTING AND A COMPUTER ILLUSTRATION TO SHOW HOW DIFFERENT MEDIA WOULD REPRODUCE ON THE PAPER GRADES. (USA)

● 254 «DER KOPFSPRUNG» (ST. SAPHORIN). DAS BILD GEHÖRT ZU EINER IN EINEM BUCH VERÖFFENTLICHTEN PHOTOREIHE ÜBER DIE SCHWEIZ, IN DER DIE MÖGLICHKEITEN DER MONTAGETECHNIK GEZEIGT WERDEN. (SWI)

● 255 AUFNAHME FÜR DEN UMSCHLAG EINES PAPIERMUSTERKATALOGS. DER AUFTRAG VER-LANGTE EINE KOMBINATION VON SCHWARZ-WEISS- UND FARBPHOTOGRAPHIE MIT EINEM BILD UND EINER COMPUTERILLUSTRATION, UM ZU ZEIGEN, WIE DIE VERSCHIEDENEN TECHNI-KEN AUF DEM PAPIER WIRKEN. (USA)

▲ 254 «LE PLONGEON». D'UNE SÉRIE PUBLIÉE DANS UN LIVRE SUR LA SUISSE UTILISANT LA TECHNIQUE DU MONTAGE PHOTOGRAPHIQUE, AFIN DE CRÉER DES IMAGES ONIRIQUES QUI DONNENT L'ILLUSION DE LA RÉALITÉ. (SWI)

▲ 255 COUVERTURE D'UN CATALOGUE D'ÉCHAN-TILLONS D'UN FABRICANT DE PAPIERS SPÉCI-AUX. IL S'AGISSAIT DE COMBINER LE NOIR ET BLANC ET LA PEINTURE AVEC UNE ILLUSTRA-TION RÉALISÉE SUR ORDINATEUR, AFIN DE CONFRONTER LES QUALITÉS D'IMPRESSION DE DIVERSES TECHNIQUES. (USA)

INDEX

VERZEICHNIS

INDEX

CALL FOR ENTRIES

GRAPHIS DESIGN 94

ENTRY DEADLINE: NOVEMBER 30, 1992

ADVERTISING: Newspaper and magazine. **DESIGN:** Promotion brochures, catalogs, invitations, record covers, announcements, logos, corporate campaigns, calendars, books, book covers, packaging (single or series, labels or complete packages). **EDITORIAL:** Company magazines, newspapers, consumer magazines, house organs, annual reports. **ILLUSTRATION:** All categories, black-and-white or color. **ELIGIBILITY:** All work produced between December 1, 1991 and November 30, 1992, including unpublished work by professionals or students.

GRAPHIS PHOTO 93

ENTRY DEADLINE: AUGUST 31, 1992

ADVERTISING PHOTOGRAPHY: Ads, catalogs, invitations, announcements, record covers and calendars on any subject. **EDITORIAL PHOTOGRAPHY:** Photos subject for journals, books and corporate publications. **FINE ART PHOTOGRAPHY:** Personal studies on any subject. **UNPUBLISHED PHOTOGRAPHS:** Experimental or student work on any subject. **ELIGIBILITY:** All work produced between Sept. 1, 1991 and Aug. 31, 1992.

GRAPHIS POSTER 94

ENTRY DEADLINE: APRIL 30, 1993

CULTURAL POSTERS: Exhibitions, film, music and theater. **ADVERTISING POSTERS:** Consumer goods and self-promotion. **SOCIAL POSTERS:** Education, conferences, political issues. **ELIGIBILITY:** All work produced between May 1, 1992 and April 30, 1993.

GRAPHIS ANNUAL REPORTS 4

ENTRY DEADLINE: APRIL 30, 1993

All annual reports, brochures, and other corporate collateral material. **ELIGIBILITY:** Work published between May 1, 1991 and April 30, 1993.

RULES

By submitting work, the sender grants permission for it to be published in any Graphis book, any article in Graphis magazine, or any advertisement, brochure or other printed matter produced specifically for the purpose of promoting the sale of these publications.

■ **ELIGIBILITY:** All work produced in the 12-month period previous to the submission deadline, including unpublished work by professionals or students, is eligible.

■ **WHAT TO SEND:** Please send the printed piece (unmounted but well protected). Do not send original art. For large, bulky or valuable pieces, please submit color photos or duplicate transparencies. We regret that entries cannot be returned.

■ **HOW AND WHERE TO SEND:** Please tape (do not glue) the completed entry form (or a copy) to the back of each piece. Entries can be sent by air mail, air parcel post or surface mail. Please do not send anything by air freight. Write "No Commercial Value" on the package, and label it "Art for Contest." The number of photographs and transparencies enclosed should also be marked on the parcel. (If sending by air courier—Federal Express or DHL, for instance—label the package "Documents, Commercial Value $00.00".) For entries from countries with exchange controls, please contact us.

■ **SINGLE ENTRIES:** North America, U.S. $15; Germany, DM 15, All other countries, SFr 15.

■ **FOR AN ENTRY OF THREE OR MORE PIECES IN A SINGLE CONTEST:** North America, U.S. $35, Germany DM 40, All other countries SFr 40.

■ **STUDENTS' ENTRIES:** Free with copy of student identification.

Please make checks payable to **GRAPHIS PRESS CORP., ZÜRICH,** and include in parcel. A confirmation of receipt will be sent to each entrant, and all entrants will be notified whether their work has been accepted for publication. By submitting work, you qualify for a 25 percent discount on the purchase of the published book. Please send entries to:

GRAPHIS PRESS CORP., 107 DUFOURSTRASSE · CH-8008 ZÜRICH, SWITZERLAND

ENTRY LABEL

SENDER:

FIRM, ADDRESS, TELEPHONE

ART DIRECTOR:

NAME, CITY, STATE

DESIGNER:

NAME, CITY, STATE

ILLUSTRATOR, PHOTOGRAPHER, STYLIST:

NAME, CITY, STATE

COPYWRITER:

NAME, CITY, STATE

AGENCY, STUDIO:

NAME, CITY, STATE

CLIENT, PUBLISHER:

NAME, CITY, STATE

DESCRIPTION OF ASSIGNMENT/OTHER INFORMATION:

SIGNATURE:

I HEREBY GRANT **GRAPHIS PRESS** NON-EXCLUSIVE PERMISSION FOR USE OF THE SUBMITTED MATERIAL, FOR WHICH I HAVE FULL REPRODUCTION RIGHTS (COPY, PHOTOGRAPHY, ILLUSTRATION, AND DESIGN).

ETIKETT/FICHE

ABSENDER/ENVOYÉ PAR:

FIRM, ADDRESS, TELEPHONE

ART DIRECTOR/DIRECTEUR ARTISTIQUE:

NAME, CITY, STATE

GESTALTER/DESIGNER:

NAME, CITY, STATE

KÜNSTLER/ARTISTE, PHOTOGRAPH(E), STYLIST/STYLISTE:

NAME, CITY, STATE

TEXTER/RÉDACTEUR:

NAME, CITY, STATE

AGENTUR/AGENCE:

NAME, CITY, STATE

KUNDE/CLIENT:

NAME, CITY, STATE

ZWECK/UTILISATION:

INFORMATION

UNTERSCHRIFT/SIGNATURE:

ICH ERTEILE HIERMIT DEM **GRAPHIS VERLAG** DIE NICHT-EXKLUSIVE ERLAUBNIS ZUR VERÖFFENTLICHUNG DER EINGEREICHTEN ARBEITEN, FÜR DIE ICH DIE REPRODUKTIONSRECHTE BESITZE (TEXT, PHOTOGRAPHIE, ILLUSTRATION UND DESIGN).

J'ACCORDE PAR LA PRÉSENTE AUX **EDITIONS GRAPHIS** L'AUTORISATION NON EXCLUSIVE D'UTILISER LE MATÉRIEL SOUMIS À LEUR APPRÉCIATION, POUR LEQUEL JE DÉTIENS LES DROITS DE REPRODUCTION (TEXTE, PHOTOGRAPHIE, ILLUSTRATION ET DESIGN).

GRAPHIS PRESS CORP., 107 DUFOURSTRASSE CH-8008 ZÜRICH, SWITZERLAND

EINLADUNG

GRAPHIS DESIGN 94

EINSENDESCHLUSS: 30. NOVEMBER 1992

WERBUNG: In Zeitungen und Zeitschriften. DESIGN: Werbeprospekte, Kataloge, Einladungen, Schallplattenhüllen, Anzeigen, Signete, Image-Kampagnen, Kalender, Bücher, Buchumschläge, Packungen. REDAKTIONELLES DESIGN: Firmenpublikationen, Zeitungen, Zeitschriften, Jahresberichte. ILLUSTRATIONEN: Alle Kategorien, schwarzweiss oder farbig. IN FRAGE KOMMEN: Alle Arbeiten von Fachleuten und Studenten – auch nicht publizierte Arbeiten –, die zwischen Dezember 1991 und November 1992 entstanden sind.

GRAPHIS PHOTO 93

EINSENDESCHLUSS: 31. AUGUST 1992

WERBUNG: Anzeigen, Prospekte, Kataloge, Einladungen, Plattenhüllen, Kalender. REDAKTIONELLE PHOTOGRAPHIE: Pressephotos, Firmenpublikationen usw. KÜNSTLERISCHE PHOTOGRAPHIE: Persönliche Studien. UNVERÖFFENTLICHTE PHOTOS: Experimentelle Photographie und Arbeiten von Studenten. IN FRAGE KOMMEN: Arbeiten, die zwischen September 1991 und August 1992 entstanden sind.

GRAPHIS POSTER 94

EINSENDESCHLUSS: 30. APRIL 1993

KULTUR: Plakate für Ausstellungen, Film-, Theater- und Balletaufführungen. WERBUNG: Plakate für Konsumgüter, Eigenwerbung GESELLSCHAFT: Ausbildung, Politik, Umwelt IN FRAGE KOMMEN: Arbeiten, die zwischen Mai 1992 und April 1993 entstanden sind.

GRAPHIS ANNUAL REPORTS 4

EINSENDESCHLUSS: 30. APRIL 1993

Alle Jahresberichte einer Firma oder Organisation. IN FRAGE KOMMEN: Arbeiten, publiziert zwischen Mai 1991 und April 1993.

TEILNAHMEBEDINGUNGEN

Durch Ihre Einsendung erteilen Sie dem Graphis Verlag die Erlaubnis zur Veröffentlichung der Arbeiten in den Graphis-Büchern und in der Zeitschrift *Graphis* oder für die Wiedergabe im Zusammenhang mit Besprechungen und Werbematerial für Graphis-Publikationen.

■ IN FRAGE KOMMEN: Alle Arbeiten von Fachleuten und Studenten – auch nicht publizierte Arbeiten –, die in der angegebenen Periode vor Einsendeschluss entstanden sind.

■ WAS EINSENDEN: Senden Sie uns das gedruckte Beispiel (gut geschützt). Senden Sie keine Originale. Bei unhandlichen, umfangreichen und wertvollen Sendungen bitten wir um Farbphotos oder Duplikat-Dias. **Bitte beachten Sie, dass Einsendungen nicht zurückgeschickt werden können.**

■ WIE SCHICKEN: Befestigen Sie das ausgefüllte Etikett (oder eine Kopie) mit Klebstreifen (nicht mit Klebstoff) auf der Rückseite jeder Arbeit. Bitte per Luftpost oder auf normalem Postweg einsenden.

Keine Luftfrachtsendungen. Deklarieren Sie «ohne jeden Handelswert» und «Arbeitsproben». Die Anzahl der Dias und Photos sollte auf dem Paket angegeben werden. Bei Luftkurier-Sendungen vermerken Sie «Dokumente, ohne jeden Handelswert».

■ GEBÜHREN: SFr. 15.–/DM 15,– für einzelne Arbeiten, SFr. 40.–/DM 40,– pro Kampagne oder Serie von mehr als drei Stück.

■ STUDENTEN: Diese Gebühren gelten nicht für Studenten. Senden Sie uns bitte eine Kopie des Studentenausweises.

Bitte senden Sie uns einen Scheck (SFr.-Schecks bitte auf eine Schweizer Bank ziehen) oder überweisen Sie den Betrag auf PC Zürich 80-23071-9 oder PSchK Frankfurt 3000 57-602. Jeder Einsender erhält eine Empfangsbestätigung und wird über Erscheinen oder Nichterscheinen seiner Arbeit informiert. Durch Ihre Einsendung erhalten Sie 25% Rabatt auf das betreffende Buch. Bitte senden Sie Ihre Arbeit an folgende Adresse:

GRAPHIS VERLAG, DUFOURSTRASSE 107, CH-8008 ZURICH, SCHWEIZ

APPEL D'ENVOIS

GRAPHIS DESIGN 94

DATE LIMITE D'ENVOI: 30 NOVEMBRE 1992

PUBLICITÉ: journaux, magazines. **DESIGN:** brochures, catalogues, invitations, pochettes de disque, annonces, logos, campagnes d'identité visuelle, calendriers, livres, jaquettes, packaging (spécimen ou série, étiquettes ou emballages complets). **DESIGN ÉDITORIAL:** magazines de sociétés, journaux, revues, publications d'entreprise, rapports annuels. **ILLUSTRATION:** toutes catégories noir et blanc ou couleurs. **ADMISSION:** tous travaux réalisés entre le 1er décembre 1991 et le 30 novembre 1992, y compris les inédits de professionnels ou d'étudiants.

GRAPHIS PHOTO 93

DATE LIMITE D'ENVOI: 31 AOUT 1992

PHOTO PUBLICITAIRE: publicités, catalogues, invitations, annonces, pochettes de disque et calendriers sur tous sujets. **PHOTO RÉDACTIONNELLE:** reportages pour périodiques, livres et publications d'entreprise. **PHOTO D'ART:** études personnelles. **PHOTOS INÉDITES:** travaux expérimentaux ou projets d'étudiants. **ADMISSION:** tous travaux réalisés entre le 1er septembre 1991 et le 31 août 1992.

GRAPHIS POSTER 94

DATE LIMITE D'ENVOI: 30 AVRIL 1993

AFFICHES CULTURELLES: expositions, films, musique et théâtre. **AFFICHES SOCIALES:** formation, conférences, politique. **ADMISSION:** tous travaux réalisés entre le 1er mai 1992 et le 30 avril 1993. **AFFICHES PUBLICITAIRES:** produits de consommation, autopromotion.

GRAPHIS ANNUAL REPORTS 4

DATE LIMITE D'ENVOI: 30 AVRIL 1993

Rapports annuels, brochures et tout matériel d'identité corporate. **ADMISSION:** travaux publiés entre le 1er mai 1991 et le 30 avril 1993.

RÈGLEMENT

Par votre envoi, vous donnez aux Editions Graphis l'autorisation de publier les travaux reçus dans nos livres Graphis, dans tout article du magazine Graphis ou toute publicité, brochure ou autre matériel publicitaire destiné à promouvoir la vente de ces publications.

■ **ADMISSION:** sont acceptés tous les travaux de professionnels et d'étudiants – même inédits – réalisés pendant les douze mois précédant le délai limite d'envoi.

■ **QUE NOUS ENVOYER:** un exemplaire imprimé (non monté, mais bien protégé). N'envoyez pas d'originaux. Pour les travaux de grand format, volumineux ou de valeur, veuillez envoyer des photos en couleurs ou diapos (duplicata). Les travaux ne pourront vous être retournés.

■ **COMMENT ET OÙ ENVOYER:** veuillez scotcher (ne pas coller) au dos de chaque spécimen les étiquettes (ou photocopies) dûment remplies. Envoyez les travaux par avion ou par voie de surface. Ne nous envoyez rien en fret aérien. Indiquez «Sans aucune valeur commerciale» et «Echantillons pour concours». Inscrire le nombre de diapositives et photos sur le paquet. (Pour les envois par courrier, indiquer «Documents, sans aucune valeur commerciale). Pour les envois en provenance de pays soumis au contrôle des changes, veuillez nous contacter.

■ **ENVOI D'UN SEUL TRAVAIL:** droits d'admission, SFr 15.–/US$ 15.00

■ **ENVOI D'UNE SÉRIE DE TROIS TRAVAUX OU PLUS POUR UN SEUL CONCOURS:** SFr 40.–/US 35.00

■ **ÉTUDIANTS:** les étudiants sont exemptés de la taxe d'admission. Prière de joindre une photocopie de la carte d'étudiant.

Veuillez joindre à votre envoi un chèque tiré sur une banque suisse ou verser ce montant au compte chèque postal Zurich, 80.23071.9. Nous vous ferons parvenir un accusé de réception. Tous les candidats seront informés de la parution ou non-parution de leurs travaux. Votre envoi vous vaudra une réduction de 20% sur l'annuel en question. Veuillez envoyer vos travaux à l'adresse suivante:

GRAPHIS PRESS CORP., DUFOURSTRASSE 107, CH-8008 ZURICH, SUISSE

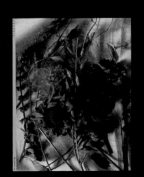

SUBSCRIBE TO GRAPHIS: USA AND CANADA

MAGAZINE	USA	CANADA

☐ NEW   ☐ RENEW

| ☐ GRAPHIS (TWO YEARS/12 ISSUES) | US $149.00 | US $166.00 |
| ☐ GRAPHIS (ONE YEAR/6 ISSUES) | US $79.00 | US $88.00 |

IMPORTANT! CHECK THE LANGUAGE VERSION DESIRED:

☐ ENGLISH   ☐ GERMAN   ☐ FRENCH

☐ CHECK ENCLOSED

☐ PLEASE BILL ME

☐ 25% DISCOUNT FOR STUDENTS WITH COPY OF VALID,
   DATED STUDENT ID AND PAYMENT WITH ORDER

FOR CREDIT CARD PAYMENT:

☐ VISA   ☐ MASTERCARD

ACCT. NO   EXP. DATE

SIGNATURE

PLEASE PRINT

NAME   DATE

TITLE

COMPANY

ADDRESS

CITY   POSTAL CODE

COUNTRY

SEND ORDER FORM AND MAKE CHECK PAYABLE TO:

GRAPHIS US, INC.,

P.O. BOX 3063

SOUTHEASTERN, PA 19398-3063

SERVICE WILL BEGIN WITH ISSUE THAT IS CURRENT

WHEN ORDER IS PROCESSED.   (PHOTO 92)

REQUEST FOR CALL FOR ENTRIES

PLEASE PUT ME ON THE "CALL FOR ENTRIES" LIST FOR THE
FOLLOWING TITLES:

☐ GRAPHIS DESIGN   ☐ GRAPHIS ANNUAL REPORTS
☐ GRAPHIS DIAGRAM   ☐ GRAPHIS CORPORATE IDENTITY
☐ GRAPHIS POSTER   ☐ GRAPHIS PACKAGING
☐ GRAPHIS PHOTO   ☐ GRAPHIS LETTERHEAD
☐ GRAPHIS LOGO   ☐ GRAPHIS TYPOGRAPHY

SUBMITTING MATERIAL TO ANY OF THE ABOVE TITLES QUALIFIES
SENDER FOR A 25% DISCOUNT TOWARD PURCHASE OF THAT TITLE.

SUBSCRIBE TO GRAPHIS: EUROPE AND WORLD

MAGAZINE	BRD	U.K.	WORLD

☐ NEW   ☐ RENEW

| ☐ GRAPHIS (TWO YEARS/12 ISSUES) | DM326,00 | £106.00 | SFR280.- |
| ☐ GRAPHIS (ONE YEAR/6 ISSUES) | DM181,00 | £ 63.00 | SFR156.- |

IMPORTANT! CHECK THE LANGUAGE VERSION DESIRED:

☐ ENGLISH   ☐ GERMAN   ☐ FRENCH

☐ SUBSCRIPTION FEES INCLUDE POSTAGE TO ANY
   PART OF THE WORLD

| ☐ AIRMAIL SURCHARGES (PER YEAR) | DM75,00 | £26.00 | SFR65.- |
| ☐ REGISTERED MAIL (PER YEAR) | DM20,00 | £ 7.00 | SFR17.- |

☐ CHECK ENCLOSED (PLEASE MAKE SFR.- CHECK PAYABLE
   TO A SWISS BANK.

☐ STUDENTS MAY REQUEST A 25% DISCOUNT BY SENDING STUDENT ID

FOR CREDIT CARD PAYMENT (ALL CARDS DEBITED IN SWISS FRANCS):

☐ AMERICAN EXPRESS   ☐ DINER'S CLUB
☐ EURO/MASTERCARD   ☐ VISA/BARCLAY/CARTE BLEUE

ACCT. NO   EXP. DATE

SIGNATURE

PLEASE PRINT

NAME   DATE

TITLE

COMPANY

ADDRESS

CITY   POSTAL CODE

COUNTRY

SEND ORDER FORM AND MAKE CHECK PAYABLE TO:

GRAPHIS PRESS CORP

DUFOURSTRASSE 107

CH-8008 ZÜRICH, SWITZERLAND

SERVICE WILL BEGIN WITH ISSUE THAT IS CURRENT

WHEN ORDER IS PROCESSED.

REQUEST FOR CALL FOR ENTRIES

PLEASE PUT ME ON THE "CALL FOR ENTRIES" LIST FOR THE
FOLLOWING TITLES:

☐ GRAPHIS DESIGN   ☐ GRAPHIS ANNUAL REPORTS
☐ GRAPHIS DIAGRAM   ☐ GRAPHIS CORPORATE IDENTITY
☐ GRAPHIS POSTER   ☐ GRAPHIS PACKAGING
☐ GRAPHIS PHOTO   ☐ GRAPHIS LETTERHEAD
☐ GRAPHIS LOGO   ☐ GRAPHIS TYPOGRAPHY

SUBMITTING MATERIAL TO ANY OF THE ABOVE TITLES QUALIFIES
SENDER FOR A 25% DISCOUNT TOWARD PURCHASE OF THAT TITLE.

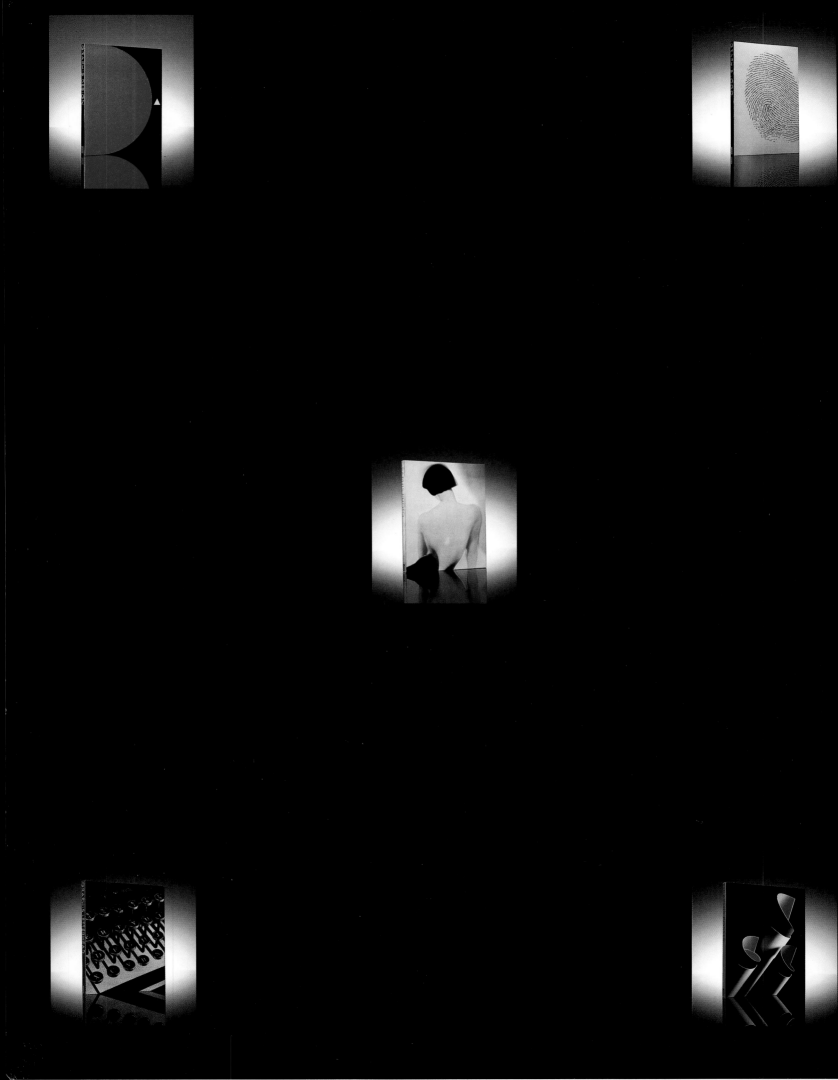

BOOK ORDER FORM: USA AND CANADA

BOOKS	USA	CANADA
☐ GRAPHIS DESIGN 92	US $69.00	US $94.00
☐ GRAPHIS DESIGN 91	US $69.00	US $94.00
☐ GRAPHIS POSTER 92	US $69.00	US $94.00
☐ GRAPHIS POSTER 91	US $69.00	US $94.00
☐ GRAPHIS PHOTO 91	US $69.00	US $94.00
☐ GRAPHIS ANNUAL REPORTS 3	US $75.00	US$100.00
☐ GRAPHIS LETTERHEAD 1	US $69.00	US $94.00
☐ GRAPHIS LOGO 1	US $50.00	US $70.00
☐ THE GRAPHIC DESIGNER'S GREENBOOK	US $25.00	US $41.00
☐ GRAPHIS PUBLICATION 1 (ENGLISH)	US $75.00	US$100.00
☐ ART FOR SURVIVAL: THE ILLUSTRATOR AND THE ENVIRONMENT	US $40.00	US $60.00
GRAPHIS CORPORATE IDENTITY 1	US $75.00	US$100.00
☐ GRAPHIS PACKAGING 5	US $75.00	US$100.00
☐ GRAPHIS DIAGRAM 1	US $69.00	US $94.00

☐ CHECK ENCLOSED (GRAPHIS AGREES TO PAY MAILING COSTS)

☐ PLEASE BILL ME (MAILING COSTS IN ADDITION TO ABOVE BOOK PRICES WILL BE CHARGED. BOOK(S) WILL BE SENT WHEN PAYMENT IS RECEIVED)

PLEASE PRINT

NAME _____ DATE _____

TITLE _____

COMPANY _____

ADDRESS _____

CITY _____ POSTAL CODE _____

COUNTRY _____

DATE _____ SIGNATURE _____

SEND ORDER FORM AND MAKE CHECK PAYABLE TO:
GRAPHIS US, INC.,
141 LEXINGTON AVENUE,
NEW YORK, NY 10016, USA

REQUEST FOR CALL FOR ENTRIES
PLEASE PUT ME ON YOUR "CALL FOR ENTRIES" LIST FOR THE FOLLOWING TITLES:

☐ GRAPHIS DESIGN	☐ GRAPHIS ANNUAL REPORTS
☐ GRAPHIS DIAGRAM	☐ GRAPHIS CORPORATE IDENTITY
☐ GRAPHIS POSTER	☐ GRAPHIS PACKAGING
☐ GRAPHIS PHOTO	☐ GRAPHIS LETTERHEAD
☐ GRAPHIS LOGO	☐ GRAPHIS TYPOGRAPHY

SUBMITTING MATERIAL TO ANY OF THE ABOVE TITLES QUALIFIES SENDER FOR A 25% DISCOUNT TOWARD PURCHASE OF THAT TITLE.

BOOK ORDER FORM: EUROPE AND WORLD

BOOKS	BRD	U.K.	WORLD
☐ GRAPHIS DESIGN 92	DM149,00	£49.00	SFR.123.-
☐ GRAPHIS DESIGN 91	DM149,00	£49.00	SFR.123.-
☐ GRAPHIS POSTER 92	DM149,00	£49.00	SFR.123.-
☐ GRAPHIS POSTER 91	DM149,00	£49.00	SFR.123.-
☐ GRAPHIS PHOTO 91	DM149,00	£49.00	SFR.123.-
☐ GRAPHIS ANNUAL REPORTS 3	DM162,00	£52.00	SFR.137.-
☐ GRAPHIS LETTERHEAD 1	DM149,00	£49.00	SFR.123.-
☐ GRAPHIS LOGO 1	DM108,00	£36.00	SFR. 92.-
☐ THE GRAPHIC DESIGNER'S GREENBOOK	DM 54,00	£18.00	SFR. 46.-
☐ GRAPHIS PUBLICATION 1 (ENGLISH)	DM162,00	£52.00	SFR.137.-
☐ ART FOR SURVIVAL: THE ILLUSTRATOR AND THE ENVIRONMENT	DM 89,00	£33.00	SFR. 79.-
☐ GRAPHIS CORPORATE IDENTITY 1	DM160,00	£48.00	SFR.132.-
☐ GRAPHIS PACKAGING 5	DM160,00	£48.00	SFR.132.-
☐ GRAPHIS DIAGRAM 1	DM138,00	£49.00	SFR.112.-

☐ CHECK ENCLOSED (PLEASE MAKE CHECK PAYABLE TO EUROPEAN BOOK SERVICE, DE MEERN)

☐ PLEASE BILL ME (MAILING COSTS WILL BE CHARGED)

FOR CREDIT CARD PAYMENT (ALL CARDS DEBITED IN SWISS FRANCS):

☐ AMERICAN EXPRESS   ☐ DINER'S CLUB

☐ EURO/MASTERCARD   ☐ VISA/BARCLAY/CARTE BLEUE

ACCOUNT NO. _____ EXPIRATION DATE _____

SIGNATURE _____ DATE _____

PLEASE PRINT

NAME _____ DATE _____

TITLE _____

COMPANY _____

ADDRESS _____

CITY _____ POSTAL CODE _____

COUNTRY _____

DATE _____ SIGNATURE _____

PLEASE SEND ORDER FORM TO:
GRAPHIS PRESS CORP.,
DUFOURSTRASSE 107,
CH-8008 ZÜRICH, SWITZERLAND

REQUEST FOR CALL FOR ENTRIES
PLEASE PUT ME ON YOUR "CALL FOR ENTRIES" LIST FOR THE FOLLOWING TITLES:

☐ GRAPHIS DESIGN	☐ GRAPHIS ANNUAL REPORTS
☐ GRAPHIS DIAGRAM	☐ GRAPHIS CORPORATE IDENTITY
☐ GRAPHIS POSTER	☐ GRAPHIS PACKAGING
☐ GRAPHIS PHOTO	☐ GRAPHIS LETTERHEAD
☐ GRAPHIS LOGO	☐ GRAPHIS TYPOGRAPHY

SUBMITTING MATERIAL TO ANY OF THE ABOVE TITLES QUALIFIES SENDER FOR A 25% DISCOUNT TOWARD PURCHASE OF THAT TITLE.

PHOTOGRAPH BY JAVIER VALLHONRAT